AF522078

Acquisition of English Vocabulary

ACQUISITION OF ENGLISH VOCABULARY

By

Dr. M. Eva Sundari Elizabeth

B.Sc., M.A., M.Ed., Ph.D.

Lecturer in English

R.V.R. College of Education

Guntur–522006

Editor

Dr. Digumarti Bhaskara Rao

M.Sc., M.A., M.A., M.Ed., Ph.D.

Reader

R.V.R. College of Education

Srinivasa Nagar Colony

Guntur–522006

and

Member, Board of Studies in Education

Acharya Nagarjuna University

Acharya Nagarjuna Nagar–522510

Andhra Pradesh (India)

DISCOVERY PUBLISHING HOUSE

NEW DELHI

Published by:
Namit Wasan

DISCOVERY PUBLISHING HOUSE PVT. LTD.
4383/4B, Ansari Road, Darya Ganj
New Delhi-110 002 (India)
Phone : +91-11-23279245; 23253475; 43596065
E-mail : discoverybooksindia@gmail.com
discoverypublishinghouse@gmail.com
namitwasan9@gmail.com
web : www.discoverypublishinggroup.com

***Edition:* 2020**

ISBN: 978-81-8356-075-7

Acquisition of English Vocabulary

Printed at:
Infinity Imaging Systems
Delhi

Preface

Language makes the people interact well and realize their objectives to their satisfaction. The vocabulary of any language is dependent on the exposure of an individual to that language and is influenced by certain factors.

Considering the very importance of the English vocabulary, a research study has been taken up and the results of the study are interesting and useful to curriculum specialists and language arts teachers.

Eva

Contents

Introduction

1

The human world is filled with people speaking different languages. Language skills form an important aspect of the growth and development of any individual. Language links people in the society through the oral form, the aural-oral skills and the written form, reading and writing. If an individual is taken away from the society and is brought up in a forest, there may be physical growth but as there is no language around except for the cries of the animals, he would also utter the cries but not meaningful sounds. Even in the society, if the child is nurtured by one who is dumb and communicates with the child through signs, the child will also not be capable of making meaningful sounds. Language develops in the society when it is spoken by people.

Any language is made up of certain elements. Language is a system comprising the elements like sound system—phonology and the structural or the grammatical elements, and lexical elements or vocabulary. Vocabulary development must be seen as an organic part of a language system involving speaking and listening, reading and writing, visualizing and observing. Student interest and ultimately motivation is a significant factor governing the success of a vocabulary programme. The early environment (experiences, encouragements, models) plays a key role in the language development, conceptual learning self image and motivational pattern of the child's intellectual growth. When provided with rich environmental experiences, the student is able to develop a stock of words. Inadequate vocabulary skills results in inadequate conceptualisation.

Experiments have shown that vocabulary size is probably the best single index for predicting achievement in nearly all the other language skills. In addition the listening vocabulary is the basis for the development of the other vocabularies. Children will not frequently use words in their speaking or writing vocabularies that they do not already understand. The words that they have heard and understand form the basis for the speaking, writing and reading that they would do. Thus the larger the size of the understanding vocabulary, the richer the foundation on which these other vocabularies can be built.

In several areas one single language is often used as a link language or lingua franca. English has been playing the role of a link language in India. It is the language of the source of knowledge. The need and importance of learning the language has been stressed by numerous people. A great orientalist and a Sanskrit scholar, Joshi (1986: p. 195) on the occasion of his felicitation by the citizens of his town—Wai, on his 86th birthday, in his speech dealt about the place of English in the process of acquisition of new knowledge, and said that the source of new knowledge has always been the West, and as we are more familiar with English language it has been our principal medium for new knowledge.

The Need for Teaching English

The Report of the Kothari Commission (1966 : p. 192) observes "a working knowledge of English will be a valuable asset for all students". Former Prime Minister, Morarji Desai (1978) said in Delhi while talking to Mr. Callaghan—the former British Prime Minister, "We will not deny to ourselves the practical as well as cultural benefits of familiarity with English, the most eloquent and popular language". Similarly the other Prime Ministers of India namely Jawahar Lal Nehru and Indira Gandhi, stressed the need and importance of English language.

The importance of English as a library language is best described by the Radha Krishnan Commission (1949) in the Report of the University Education Commission: 1948-49 p. 325] — "English however must continue to be studied. It is a language which is rich in literature, humanistic, scientific and technical knowledge. If under sentimental urges we should give up English, we would cut ourselves from the living stream of ever growing knowledge". The Official Language Commission (1950) appointed by the Government of India states — "since we need knowledge of English for different purposes, the content and character of that language as well as the method of imparting it have to undergo changes. English has to be taught hereafter, principally as a language of comprehension rather than as literary language so as to develop in the students learning of it, a faculty for comprehending writings in the English language, more especially those relating to the subject matter of their specialised fields of studies".

A study conducted by Shaw (1979) on students from Hyderabad city in India revealed that the students studied English because they would need it for jobs, and it was required in the system of education. The students felt strongly that the English language made them better persons. The results of the study indicated that most of the students had a positive attitude towards the learning of English. From the reasons given by the students it can be said that students were generally learning English for instrumental purposes. If the language is being used for such a purpose to fulfil an educational requirement, to get a better position and to read material in the language, then it is being learnt for instrumental purposes.

In India there are large enrollments in English medium schools or English subject classes, in spite of the switchover of the medium of instruction from English to the regional languages in most of the Universities. A few states namely Uttar Pradesh, Madhya Pradesh and Bihar have discontinued the use of English at the High School stage while the other states retained English as a compulsory subject of study upto the graduate level with the view that the study of English helps the students going for higher education like post-graduation and professional courses such as Medicine, Engineering and Law.

In Andhra Pradesh English is the third language at the High School stage and second language at the intermediate and graduate level. English is taught and learnt in the schools for a period of five to six years from class V.

The Objectives of Teaching English at School Levels

The general objectives of teaching English are four-fold namely, to develop listening comprehension, speaking ability, reading comprehension and writing ability. Of these four, reading comprehension is to be emphasized more as recommended by the Official Language Commission and the Kothari Commission. English is to be taught in our schools as a language of comprehension. But the reading comprehension cannot be taught in isolation. The Psychology of language learning tells us that the four basic skills namely listening, speaking, reading and writing, reinforce each other, and even if a single skill is to be developed some amount of emphasis on other skills is beneficial. In the broadest terms the following are the objectives:

(a) To understand English with ease when spoken at normal speed.

(b) To speak English correctly and fluently with proper stress and intonation.

(c) To read English with comprehension and reasonable speed so as to use it as a library language for collecting information and for enjoyment.

(d) To write neatly and correctly at reasonable speed.

(e) To enjoy simple poems in English.

(f) To acquire knowledge of the elements of English for practical command of the language.

(g) To translate common English words and phrases and sentences into their functional equivalents in mother tongue and vice versa.

(h) To develop an interest in English.

These objectives are expected to make the student use English effectively in ordinary every day situations by the time the student leaves the secondary school. The every day situations could be ordinary conversations, listening to English news and other programmes over the radio, reading and understanding English news items in Newspapers and Journals, enjoying simple poems, writing personal letters, applications and reports, etc., in English.

VOCABULARY

Language material consists of words and sentences. Words are to be mastered to get good vocabulary. There are over half a million words listed in the Oxford English Dictionary. It is highly impossible for anyone to know or use all those words. Fowler (1965) remarked that the power of choosing different ways of saying the same thing is a great gift of civilisation. But the Indian situation in regional language schools demands that the students should be taught the best and the most useful way of saying anything in English. It is stated by the language experts that the student of secondary school who is studying English as a third language (or second language) should master about 275 syntactic structures and about 3,000 words.

These syntactic structures and words are introduced step by step through the English Readers of classes V to X. Supplementary readers are also recommended for extensive reading to reinforce the words they already learnt from the reader and at the same time to introduce a few new words also. The range of words known to a person is known as his vocabulary. To be fluent in any skill, a good vocabulary is essential. Written or oral communication is best done with the knowledge and understanding of the use of vocabulary.

Vocabulary is an integral part of learning with all reading materials.

Every individual possesses four types of vocabularies—Listening vocabulary, Speaking vocabulary, Reading vocabulary and Writing vocabulary. One can manage to speak with minimum words and still be understood. But as a listener one has to know more words since the person to whom he is listening may use any word in the language. A listener has a more urgent need for vocabulary development. Similarly one can write with the help of a few words but while reading one faces numerous words. The meaning of the words can be understood by the context, but still for the exact meaning one would need to go to the dictionary. For most of the people, looking into the dictionary once is not enough to fix a word permanently in the mind. Constant reference to the dictionary or even constant interruptions to guess again at the same old word, makes reading slow and reduces the speed of going through the text. Hence there is a need to master more number of words to read quickly and easily.

In English there are two types of words—the structural words and the content words. The structural words are the functional words which express the relation of grammatical structures. The articles, auxiliaries, prepositions, pronouns, conjunctions, interrogatives and indefinite substitute words are very important for the construction of sentences. The content words are the words that stand for things, actions and qualities. These words are picturable. The content words may be grouped under four broad classes corresponding with the traditional parts of speech namely nouns, verbs, adjectives and adverbs. The total number of structural words are 300 and the rest of the words are content words. To frame a sentence both structural and content words are essential.

Teachers and students of English language should have a concern for vocabulary and syntax. To construct a sentence one has to know the meaning of words and the usage of the words. The vocabulary is determined by the richness and depth of one's reading and writing experience which are influenced by his/her environment. The environment can be changed to increase the experiences. The prime method of promoting growth in children's vocabulary is the enrichment of experience both actual and vicarious.

Vicarious experiences too extend and deepen children's understanding as they listen to stories and explanations, watch television or films, read books, study pictures in their books, listen to the radio or recordings and read verse and stories. Although such experiences are a source of additional ideas of words for expressing them, the pupils can derive full benefit only if they have the opportunity to discuss these ideas and clarify and correct the impressions. They need someone who is proficient in the English language to talk over these experiences or to tell these experiences.

Krashen (1979) in his discussion of methodology and his Monitor model, states that "current position is that more vocabulary means more comprehension of input, which in turn means more acquisition of syntax". He speaks of optimal input i.e., input at an appropriate level just beyond the learners' current linguistic competence. Intake should not only be comprehensible, but should also contain enough new linguistic data so that the creative construction process continues to be stimulated. The same can be said about English vocabulary. If students receive enough of this input and if the barriers to learning caused by fear and anxiety are subdued they will acquire many English words. The input hypotheses clearly states that our classtime, materials, syllabus and teaching should be solely geared to providing the students with comprehensible input with a bit of cosmetic conscious learning. The lowering of nervous tension often associated with language learning must be seen as essentially humane and beneficial in any educational setting.

Large exposure may aid language acquisition which in turn is likely to increase vocabulary. A favourable disposition towards the language and culture might be conducive and necessary to successful language acquisition. The favourable dispositions toward the language learning and other cultures which are conducive to second/third language learning are transmitted through the family. These favourable attitudes are often dependent on socio-economic conditions and family orientations.

Vocabulary plays an important role in communication. Vocabulary is necessary for reading comprehension. Not being able to find the right words is the most frustrating experience. Vocabulary is an important aspect of knowledge. The knowledge of a person depends on the bulk of vocabulary that one possesses. The success of an individual is governed by his vocabulary. For the Indian students mastery of vast vocabulary in English is likely to be an asset in their higher education and might be useful in their professional life. In the initial stages of learning a language, one gets acquainted only with words and not sentences.

The stock of words might give one the confidence to express his feelings, ideas etc. in the language. Hence there is a need to pay attention to the development of vocabulary. The learner, many a time, struggles to express well because of the inability to recall the right word. The learner might have a concept in mind but may be at a loss to recall the appropriate word while quoting Dippie, Sachdev (1977) reported that "words are like bottles and contain ideas just as bottles contain medicines". Words are the most important elements of social needs. Man's life depends upon the use of words. Words are very useful for self expression. Man is able to gather a vast treasure of knowledge only through words.

Contributing Factors for Language/Vocabulary Learning

In view of the importance of vocabulary in the learning of a language, special attention must be given to this skill. It is worthwhile to look into the factors that influence the development of English vocabulary.

For the majority of the Indian students who are getting school education in their mother tongue (regional language), the English class in the school is likely to be the only place for listening to English. Outside the English class the student has contact with the local language. This means the English teacher has an important role to play in the learning of English words. The students depend on the teacher for clear guidance and attractive measures in teaching/learning new vocabulary. In case the English teacher converts the class into a translation class the students would get almost nothing out of it. The more English words the teacher uses the better equipped will the students be. In other words, the more the input from the English teacher, the better may be the output of the student and the more may be the learning.

Next to school, home is the place where the learner learns or unlearns what he has learnt. The parents may contribute to the vocabulary acquisition directly or indirectly. If the parents are well educated they may supervise their children's study and also help in solving their problems in meaning, spelling and usage of words that are new and difficult.

The socio-economic status of parents may also be a factor which contributes to the student's vocabulary development. The parents of high and middle socio-economic status can perhaps place before the children, the audio-visual equipment like radio, tape recorder or a television. Very informally the children may be influenced by the audio-visual equipment and children may pick up English words from the programme that they hear over a radio or television. A parent may provide all varieties of toys—some of which are educative in nature, such as word building sets or puzzles. Some parents take interest in their children's education and engage tutors for difficult subjects like Mathematics, English and Science. Parents who can afford to pay for their children's education take better care about their studies.

Edgar Dale (1965a) presented a paper on "Vocabulary Development of the Under-privileged Child". He feels that children of the lower strata of society are not proficient in vocabulary because models of excellence in use of vocabulary or sentence structure are not available easily to these children. The children coming from under-privileged homes have lesser capacity for sustained attention. With an empty stomach or weak health they cannot keep their mind on what is going on in the class. They probably have limited opportunity to listen to a radio or a television. They do not associate with urban children. The parents of under-privileged children cannot afford to buy reading material like an English daily or English story books or cartoons, for they themselves do not read and cannot supply reading material to their children.

Reading materials, in-addition to the classroom instruction, can reinforce their vocabulary development. There is little scope for him to go to places like the zoo, or museum or to picnics. The deprived child is physically restricted in a number of things he has seen, heard, touched and tasted. He lacks perceptual experience. There is also a lack of sequencing, the giving of order to these experiences. The child lacks a satisfactory filing system for the vocabulary and syntax to store or retrieve experiences. Deutsch (1965) has pointed out that the child not only lacks perceptual experience but sustained attention as well, and the perseverance necessary to master these experiences. If an environment is set up for children, in which they can taste and touch and smell, manipulate, see, feel and work on materials, they will be able to name and label, because children learn by active contact with things that make a difference to them.

A child's own personal characteristics seem to affect his learning of English vocabulary. Intelligence may be a major factor in the acquisition of vocabulary. Children of high intelligence have the capacity to learn more. The other personal factor is the health of the child. A student who is generally in good health will not like to miss the school. On the other hand an unhealthy student may miss the school and the classes. As the other subjects are in the mother tongue the student does not find much difficulty in understanding them. English being a difficult subject, as it is a foreign language, the student finds it difficult to follow the continuation of the lessons after missing the classes. If there is no one at home to help the student to understand what he has missed because of his absence, the child feels bored due to the inability to follow.

In the rural schools the teachers complain that the children are very irregular to the school because they go for agricultural work. The parents are also not particular about sending their children to school during the harvest seasons. Inability to attend school either due to ill-health or any other reason, interrupts the children's learning.

When a child's vocabulary is developed in the classroom and the child gets guidance at home simultaneously in learning English words, the child may use his leisure time in further developing or expanding vocabulary. Some of the leisure time activities which may contribute directly or indirectly to the development of the vocabulary of the pupils are reading English story books, playing vocabulary games, singing or listening to English songs, acting in simple English skits or watching them or any such activities. The student could be a direct participant in the activity or an observer. The leisure time activities thus form vicarious experiences through which perhaps they can build their vocabulary.

The emotional state of the learner may influence the learning. If the learner is wrapped in fear and anxiety very little learning takes place or sometimes even no learning may take place. The fear or anxiety may be due to their poor achievement in the subject, or inability to follow perhaps due to continuous absence, or the teacher's use of high language or the strictness of the teacher etc. Whatever may be the reason, it may act as an obstacle in the learning of the subject.

Some children seem to be frightened of the English period and the English teacher. This fear builds up a negative attitude towards the subject—English. Such children will face the English period as if it were a big burden and as soon as the class is over they feel the burden has rolled away, and they are relieved of their tension. Such a feeling will hinder the progress of learning English words. By nature the child may not be timid, but still inside he may have this fear of the subject which blocks his acquisition of English vocabulary. Thus there may be a bunch of variables within the individual child and in his environment which may influence vocabulary acquisition of the child.

When the various factors that contribute to the development of English vocabulary are known, the learner situation can be changed to equip the student with the tasks to improve his English vocabulary. The child leaves school after class X. Before the child leaves the school, if the child is equipped with the knowledge of various factors and techniques that would improve his vocabulary, it would be beneficial to the child. Hence there is a need to study this problem at the school leaving stage, i.e., class X. Factors such as socio-economic status educational level of the parents etc. can be modified in the learner to facilitate maximum learning of English vocabulary. As such there is a need to know about the effect of those factors which influence the acquisition of English vocabulary.

The Present Study

Development of vocabulary is one of the pre-requisites for learning any language. Especially in the case of a foreign language vocabulary assumes greater importance. As it has been discussed earlier different ways and means are to be used in the Indian schools for the development of language skills, namely, listening comprehension, speaking ability, reading comprehension and writing ability. Vocabulary acquisition forms a basic requirement for the development of the above skills.

How should the skill of vocabulary acquisition be developed? What are the different factors associated with this skill? What are the possible inter-correlations among the different sets of independent variables which may influence the vocabulary acquisition? The above are some of the questions which should be answered on the basis of empirical evidence so as to improve the status of a foreign language which is being taught as a second/third language in the school education.

An analysis into the research already done in this area may help the researcher to understand more clearly the present status of English in school education. Probably some of the questions raised above may be answered even without a further investigation and a few more questions may come into existence which probably may be answered by undertaking research on a clearly stated problem in the light of the review.

However, the area of research for the present study is to study the English vocabulary acquisition of students of secondary schools and the means and methods in relation to different independent variables which may influence the acquisition of vocabulary. It is believed that this type of study may help many teachers of English to bring appropriate changes in their classroom practices of teaching English. It is also hoped that the study would throw light on the influence of different variables involved in the acquisition of English vocabulary by the secondary school students.

Resume of Succeeding Chapters

The second chapter describes the critical analysis of the review of related literature.

In the third chapter the problem is stated along with its objectives and hypotheses and also the variables included in the study.

The methods of investigation employed at various stages of the study viz., measurement of the variables, selection of the sample, collection of the data, scoring and analysis of data are described in the fourth chapter.

The fifth chapter deals with the actual analysis of the data, testing the hypotheses and drawing conclusions on the basis of major findings in the analysis.

Chapter six describes the summary of the entire investigation, implications and recommendations and also suggestions for further research.

2

Review of Related Literature

The purpose of the chapter is to know the status of research in the general field of language development and more specifically English vocabulary development which forms as a basic requirement for the development of different skills of English as a second/third language. Lot of research has been carried out on language development throughout the world. English being a link language at the international level, more concentration is shown by researchers of different countries on the development of different skills of this language among the school-going children in various countries.

The other more important reason for undertaking the critical analysis of research that has already been done in this area is to know different methods adapted by the earlier researchers in measuring various components of language development; to understand different techniques employed to identify the cause and effect relationships among the skills of language and various personal and environmental factors; to notice the variations and contradictions in the results obtained by the earlier researchers; and to know the gaps in research in this field. It is believed that the thorough knowledge of the past research would help the researcher to formulate a meaningful and useful research problem, with a clear understanding of the objectives that are to be realised, questions that are to be answered, hypotheses that are to be formulated and tested, and the intervening variables that are to be considered.

After having collected the information from different sources on the research done in the area of language development, the review is critically analysed and presented under the following sub-titles:

1. Different methods of learning vocabulary.
2. Learning of different types of words.
3. Organisation of language text—vocabulary acquisition.
4. Influence of social, psychological factors on acquisition of language skills.

Different Methods of Learning Vocabulary

Children master language by learning small words and then phrases and finally some small sentences. Thus vocabulary is the first step in learning any language. Research in vocabulary is therefore of fundamental importance. Wittrock (1986) pointed out in *The Handbook of Research on Teaching* that "there has been little systematic study of classroom vocabulary". The studies on vocabulary have been divided by him into two broad categories, namely (i) readability and (ii) context effects which means the relation between vocabulary and comprehension. Both focus on the content of instruction more than on teaching activities but many of the findings appear to have instructional implications.

From the review of the research on readability it is concluded that it is probably easier for students to make their way through a text that has common words and short sentences. From the review of research on vocabulary and comprehension it was found that "under certain circumstances a student may learn something about the meaning of a new word from reading a passage. The nature of the passage, the relation between the words and the text, the type of assessment are all candidates in determining the effectiveness of contextually based learning. We are still in the dark about the specifics of the factors" Wittrock (1986).

Most of the studies reviewed in *The Handbook of Research on Teaching* (Wittrock, 1986) showed that students could learn under a variety of conditions, given enough practice. A large number of studies have been carried out to test vocabulary of children and adults in different parts of the world.

Barnard (1961) made a study of "Pre-university (PUC) students vocabulary in Chotanagpur". In this study, she found that the difficult words were taught by translation or explanation on a single occasion. The teacher made use of Indian English. She further says that poor acquisition of vocabulary among the students was because the teachers were not teaching vocabulary as they ought to.

Clark (1973) made a study of "The Child's Acquisition of Semantics in his first language." He found that children learn the meaning of the word by adding features. According to him the word wide is incompletely understood if it is only taken to mean big because this aspect would also be a feature of tall or long. When the child adds the feature that wide refers to size on the horizontal dimension, its meaning is more nearly complete.

Jenkins, et al. (1978) conducted a study on "Vocabulary and Reading Comprehension: Instructional effects". They investigated the effects of vocabulary instruction on word knowledge and reading comprehension. The results showed that methods which used synonyms and required vocabulary mastery were superior to methods employing context.

Kotakgira (1981) conducted a research on the "Development of a course for increasing the reading proficiency in English of the post-high school students of Gujarat". The research attempted to develop an auto instructional course that would increase the reading proficiency in English of the students of post-high school stage. The course was designed on the lines of skills approach and included one unit each on the skills of word recognition, word meaning, guessing the meanings of words from the context, reading in meaningful phrases, sentence meaning, finding the main idea, using a dictionary, guided reading and speed reading with comprehension. The course was modified after the try out on 118 post-SSC on the basis of statistical data obtained, students opinion and the researchers observation during the try out.

In the modified version of the course there were eight units, the one on word recognition and dictionary use were dropped. This modified material was tried out on a sample of 233 students of class XI who volunteered to take the course. The pre-test and post-test showed that it was possible to develop the reading proficiency of the students through the skills approach in which the learner practised different skills separately before he engaged in the task of reading in its entirety. The amount of development of speed depended on how well the learner was equipped with the knowledge of the language and his style of work in general.

The perceptual exercise of recognizing words in isolation did not produce results in terms of either speed or accuracy.

Gaikwad (1982) carried on an investigation on "A comparative study of efficiency of the Direct Method and the Bilingual Method of teaching English to lower classes of secondary schools in rural areas of Maharashtra state". It was an experimental study. The investigator himself taught two separate groups through Direct method to one group and through Bilingual method to the second group.

The parallel groups experimental design was followed. Each group contained 43 pupils of which 22 were boys and 21 were girls. The groups were equated on the basis of equal number of pupils, sex, chronological age, IQ, general scholarship, SES of parents etc. The experiment was conducted for one academic year. He found from his study that the Bilingual method was superior to the Direct method in developing, the linguistic skills of understanding speaking and writing and the language elements of structure and vocabulary.

Martin (1984) has investigated into the "Advanced Vocabulary Teaching: The problem of Synonyms". The study had a two-fold aim: to help avoid the formation of incorrect hypotheses about vocabulary when it is first presented, and more importantly, to help teachers deal with errors as they occur. The author identified that vocabulary errors manifest one or more kinds of dissonance between the word and its context. According to her, the four dissonances that interfere with encoding by advanced learners are: stylistic, syntactic, collocational and semantic. To avoid errors in stylistic appropriateness in a second language the investigator states that new vocabulary should be clearly labeled as to style— formal, informal, colloquial, technical literary, archaic, regional, taboo, etc.

Students should know who would use a word in talking about what and with whom.. She strongly feels that the stylistic value of vocabulary should be an integral part of vocabulary teaching. She reports that syntactic dissonances abound in student utterances. One of the examples quoted for syntactic errors is "given worship as a general word for pray, the students immediately attached to the new word the same preposition they knew to be required with the familiar one, and began speaking of 'worshipping to God"' (Stenson, 1974). To rectify such mistakes the investigator suggested that teachers should anticipate as many as possible of the syntactic misapprehensions that might be formed when new vocabulary is equated with synonyms already familiar to students, and take time to illustrate their differing syntactic behaviours.

The quasi-fluent advanced student frequently comes with unidiomatic collocations, as in "I was a large smoker" or "the storm made a lot of damage" instead of "I was a heavy smoker and the storm did a lot of damage". It is found that errors in collocation plague the speech and writing of non-native speakers who are not fully aware of the very great number of combinations. Collocational information is a vital component in the learning of new vocabulary in a second language: one does not really "know" a word until one knows its collocational profile.

According to the author, the semantic dissonance is possibly the most complex. Semantic theory has contributed richly to the understanding of the subtle and elusive distinctions among words of similar meaning. Words can be analysed in terms of semantic features which rest on familiar concepts such as animate/inanimate, abstract/ concrete and state/event. One familiar error is the use of a semantically restricted term where a general word would have succeeded as in: "I have to rectify my younger brother, where the word 'correct' would have worked. Correct is more general and 'rectify' is more specialized. Second or foreign language instruction typically moves over time from general terms toward those with increased specificity.

The following suggestions are offered: The teacher while presenting new vocabulary in any language can (i) identify stylistic level: formal, informal, colloquial, technical etc., (ii) provide examples of the word in its major grammatical frames, contrasting it if necessary with any "synonyms" appearing in the lesson, (iii) provide its most common collocates, (iv) if the item is glossed with a "synonym", determine whether the new item is a hyponym of the old one and supply the additional information that restricts the new one.

Once the nature of the misuse is apparent, teachers can explain it to the student. Teacher should not alter the surrounding context unless the mismatch is syntactic and the word itself is desirable but, merely needs to be used in a different grammatical frame. Learners output should be respected; teachers should not make wholesale alterations on it. This kind of approach enables the students to notice the multiple factors at work in choosing words for contexts, they will begin to ask the kinds of questions that will lead them to increase proficiency in expressing meanings fluently and accurately.

Dickinson (1984) carried on an investigation on the "Children's Knowledge of words gained from a single exposure First Impressions". In this study two experiments examined factors affecting word learning. Children of the age group four to eleven were the subjects of the study. The questions taken up in the study were (a) Can school aged children form fast mapping of words heard only once in a conversation, in a story and with definitions? (b) Does context affect word learning? (c) Do first and sixth graders show same patterns of acquisition? The children were tested individually by the author in a spare room in their school and all sessions were tape recorded. They heard the words in three different conditions—a conversation, a story and the word paired with a definition.

The results indicated that children at all ages could identify new words, were sensitive to correct usage and could acquire a partial semantic representation from a single exposure. Explicit definitions were most useful to older children. This showed that meta linguistic awareness and memory strategies affect word learning. There is an evidence to suggest that meanings for new words are better learned if the exemplar is peripheral to previously named category.

Nation and Liu Na (1985) conducted a study on "Factors Affecting Guessing Vocabulary in Context". According to the investigators "guessing the meanings of words from context is the most important strategy for dealing with low frequency vocabulary in written test." The sample comprised 59 teachers of English as a second language, attending a diploma course with proficiency in English ranging from a few native speakers of English to a few who communicate and read in English with considerable difficulty. The test material had two sets of passages, each set consisted of a short passage and a long passage which contained a version of the short passage. The passage was made by replacing all the words not in the GSL with nonsense words. The subjects were asked to replace the unknown words with known words from their mother tongue or with English words or paraphrases.

The results of this research indicated that learners work as a group and share their guesses and they can successfully guess the meanings of all the words. The results offer some useful guidelines for a teacher. "The guessing strategy is best introduced as a class activity concentrating on verbs and nouns which have plenty of known surrounding context. Guessing from context is a very powerful strategy for dealing with low frequency vocabulary. It deserves a considerable amount of attention in English classes", say Nation and Liu Na (1985).

Bullard (1985) investigated into "Word based perception: a handicap in second language acquisition?" The purpose of the study was to illustrate Pollack and Pickett's findings to teachers attending seminars in the teaching of listening. Pollack and Pickett 'lifted' individual words from various samples of spoken discourse (of varying degrees of relaxedness) and played these isolated items to native speakers, who were asked to identify them. The results seemed to indicate that a capacity to understand spoken language does not call for great accuracy in the identification of the individual components of that discourse.

The subjects were teachers of English in France, who were divided into two major categories: (1) native speakers of French, teachers and proficient speakers of English and (2) native speakers of English resident in France, and therefore relatively competent speakers of French. They were administered two sets of twenty decontextualized items, one in French and one in English. The items were individual words which formed parts of recordings either of radio or TV news broadcasts. The subjects listened to the recorded items either in groups or individually.

The results indicated that subjects who spoke the language as second language were more successful than those who were native speakers. Secondly subjects tended to be more successful in their second language, than their first. In the discussion of the results, Bullard states that the subjects' superior abilities to identify words in a second language derives from the manner in which they have acquired that language. This may well be more word-oriented than the first language acquisition. It may be that second language learners have the alternative of either a word by word approach or a global strategy. In the first language the volume of input is so great that one is forced to adopt a global approach. From the teachers point of view it is important to be aware that this situation (word by word approach) exists and take steps to make the learner develop a global approach to listening.

Halverson (1985) made an investigation of "Culture and Vocabulary Acquisition". According to the investigator, "Two vital elements of effective communication in a foreign language—the understanding of foreign culture and acquisition of vocabulary in a cultural context—often receive inadequate or inappropriate attention in the class room". The goal of their investigation and proposal was to provide concrete suggestions about the effective handling of time currently available in a curriculum which hopes to produce students who are able to communicate with a more sensitive control of linguistic and cultural subtleties.

The suggestions offered are a synthesis of the teaching of culture and vocabulary, incorporation of cultural information into the vocabulary learning process. She stresses the need for presenting vocabulary in a total cultural system, so that the student can conceive a more conceptually accurate image of what the word actually means in the foreign society. Teaching of vocabulary within the framework of the foreign culture lends itself to the grouping of words into contextually related categories, context related categories allow the students to learn vocabulary more efficiently than alphabetised lists of vocabulary ordered according to grammatical function. The learning of vocabulary within a relevant cultural context is a much more enlightening and interesting experience for the student.

Jiganti and Tindall (1986) conducted an investigation into "An interactive approach to teaching vocabulary". The purpose of the study was to find an effective way to teach vocabulary and also to compare two types of classroom vocabulary instruction with a non-instruction type homework assignment. The two methods of classroom vocabulary instruction were (1) a set of categorization exercise to help the students tie new words into existing framework of knowledge and (2) dramatic interpretations of new words to encourage student involvement. These two methods were compared with non-instruction type homework assignment.

Correlation evidence pointed out that individual students were better suited to learning under one or the other classroom conditions. That is, students who retained a large number of new words under the category condition might not learn as effectively under drama conditions, while students who benefited greatly from dramatization might not be greatly influenced by categorization activities. Students who had begun to use new words in class reported that they continued to use them outside the class. The other teachers also commented that the children used these new words in their classes. Children used these new words at home and also in their vacation.

The investigators were of the opinion that classroom activities provided a better learning environment for children with lower reading levels. They found that learning under homework conditions was significantly related to prior reading achievement. Good readers learned more than poor readers when they worked alone. Whereas in the classroom activities the advantage was the same for all; both good and poor readers improved their word power.

Weiss (1986) carried on an investigation on "Differential Effects of Differing Vocabulary Presentations". The effects of differing vocabulary presentations on various vocabulary and text comprehension measures were investigated. The participants in the study were thirty-seven students enrolled in a developmental reading course at an urban University in south eastern United States. Vocabulary materials were designed to compare the effects of a definition presentation with a definition plus context presentation. The definition group was presented 25 orthographically and phonologically legal invented pseudo-words. Each pseudo-word was accompanied by a dictionary like definition. The definition context group was presented the same pseudo-words with accompanying definitions. In addition each pseudo-word was used in the context of two adjoining sentences. Subjects in the control group were presented an irrelevant list of common words with accompanying symbols. Subsequently all the groups read a stimulus passage containing the pseudo-words.

The results indicated that both the treatment groups out performed the control group on two vocabulary measures. Vocabulary training improved text comprehension. Factor analytic research accrued support for a strong relationship between vocabulary knowledge and reading comprehension. It was also found that there was significant difference among the three groups of students namely the definition group, the definition-context group and the controlled group. But further analysis revealed that two experimental groups did not differ significantly.

Coomber, Ramstad, et al. (1986) investigated on "Elaboration in vocabulary learning: A comparison of three rehearsal methods". The purpose of the study was to find out to what extent rehearsal on one type of activity led to transfer to other recall tasks, and if there was a transfer, which method could carry over more effectively to others. The sample selected comprised one hundred and thirty-four Concordia college students enrolled in Freshman classes. They were randomly assigned to one of three groups—definitions (43), examples (46) and sentence composing (45).

The two groups—one on definitions and the other on examples, were asked to write the target word beside the definitions or examples that corresponded to that particular group. The sentence writing group were asked to write a one-sentence response to each target word, using the target word in their sentence and underline it. Pretest and Post-test were conducted on all the three groups namely, definition, example and sentence writing. Appropriate statistical techniques were applied.

The analysis revealed no significant interaction, hence the remaining analysis focussed on differences among the three treatments; means and standard deviations were found. Analysis of variance was conducted to test the effects of the different treatments and post-tests.

Follow-up tests revealed that, with respect to the treatment main effect, the definitions, encoding participants did more poorly than did the sentence-composing participants. With respect to the post-test main effect, definitions were easier than both sentence composing and examples. On the definition test, analysis of variance revealed no overall significant difference. Differences between definitions and sentence composing were significant.

On the example test, analysis of variance revealed no significant differences, on the sentence composing post-test, a one way analysis of variance revealed a significant difference between treatment groups. Differences between examples and sentence-composing groups were marginally significant.

This study supports composing as an effective means of learning specified lexical items. Sentence composing participants demonstrated superior word knowledge, they had performed very well on the mode in which they had rehearsed, they also registered a significantly superior performance on the definitions test. The effectiveness of sentence composing supports elaboration and levels of processing theories in the realm of learning lexical items; the more deeply one processes lexical items the better the short term memory. The effectiveness of sentence composing as a rehearsal technique also lends further support to the generation theory proposed by Slamecka and Graf (1978) and to writing as a means of learning as stated by Emig (1977) and others.

Underwood and Scluz (1960) indicated that perhaps ten to twenty exposures are needed before a student really knows a word. Craik and Lockhart (1972) emphasized the relationship between depth of analysis and retention. Hyde and Jenkins (1969) demonstrated the validity of the basic levels of processing hypothesis, with performance on superficial tasks compared with performance requiring processing at a greater depth. "For example, students counting numbers of e's or number of letters in words in a list were less likely to recall the words than were students judging words as pleasant or unpleasant in connotation.

In another study participants who were asked to indicate whether human faces were male or female were less likely to recall those faces on post-test than were participants asked to judge those faces likeable or honest (Bower and Karlin, 1974). Slamecka and Graf (1978) found that subjects rehearsing on word completion tasks (e.g. rapid-f in a synonym completion task) retained a word list more effectively than did subjects who were simply given the synonym paid (e.g. rapid-fast). This led to the conclusion that generation "entails a more profound processing level than does the automatic act of reading" a stimulus (Slamecka and Graf, 1978).

Deighton (1960) described word-learning as concept learning, suggesting that students acquire a word's meaning gradually, in an additive fashion, with numerous "experiences" with that word. Examples could be regarded as concept building exposure to a word, opportunities for the learner to apply the word in various situations. When the student has learned the definition, he or she might try it out in different situations to see whether those situations are examples of that word. Nitsch (1977) and Divesta and

Peverly (1984) found that examples studied with definitions produced retention superior to study of definitions alone. Examples provided an effective kind of elaboration on the word meaning.

Composing is another potential elaboration's strategy. Emig (1977) proposed writing as an effective means of learning. Emig contends that writing in addition to being a primary method of communication is also a most effective means of learning, because writing calls for considerable active involvement and activates extensive cognitive processes, composing might be regarded as a very effective type of generation.

Peper and Mayer (1978) provide support to writing as a means of learning, using note-taking as their topic of investigations. Note-takers in their study outperformed non-note-takers on far transfer tasks. When asked to report what they had learnt, note-takers produced more coherent text and more idea units. Peper and Mayer explained the superior performance via generative theory, by paraphrasing, structuring and ascribing meaning to newly acquired information, the learner integrates new material into past experiences. Composing tasks call for putting the word in meaningful context, encouraging learners to draw on past experiences and make meaningful applications.

Balajthy (1988) conducted "An investigation of Learner-control variables in Vocabulary Learning using two traditional instruction and two forms of computer based instruction". The study investigated the ability of 60 college level Developmental Reading course students to monitor adequacy of vocabulary instruction in traditional workbook-like tasks, as opposed to two different computer-based formats: Video game and text game exercises. In each class session, the three groups studied fifteen vocabulary words and definitions. One small group studied the words using traditional workbook-like exercises, another group studied the same words using a computer-based vocabulary text, drill game, QUIZITY and the third group studied the same words using a computer-based vocabulary video drill game, word attack. Students were allowed to spend as much or a little time as desired to study the vocabulary under the constraints of a 60 minute maximum. The study lasted three days for each class, spaced over a two week period. On each day the students studied a different set of words and also on each day they received a lesson in each of the three instructional formats. Following the study, subjects were required to estimate the effectiveness level and interest level of each format.

The results of this study raised serious questions about the effectiveness of learner controlled instructional formats, both in traditional and in computer-based learning. Results suggested that college level developmental reading students were unable to accurately monitor the success or failure of their own vocabulary learning. The time on task measures reflected a similar inability to differentiate effective from less effective instruction. The relationship between achievement and motivation in education was not clear.

The author is of the opinion that the students in the present study may have consistently confused the motivation value of the instructional formats with the teaching effectiveness. Some of the tentative instructional applications of the present study as suggested by him are: teachers must be aware that students have difficulty in monitoring their own learning, both in traditional and in computer-based tasks. Learner control of instruction may result in adverse consequences as a result. Feedback and training of college students, with teacher monitoring their achievement can contribute to a closer monitoring of reading success and more effective application of that monitoring to classroom practice.

Reutzel and Hollingsworth (1988) conducted a study on "Highlighting key vocabulary: A generative—reciprocal procedure for teaching selected inference types". This study investigated the effectiveness of highlighting key vocabulary and of a generative reciprocal inference procedure for teaching third grade readers to make inferences. The authors assigned 71 third grade students to three blocks according to reading abilities as measured by a standardized reading achievement test.

Subjects from each block were then randomly assigned to one of three groups. In the Generative Reciprocal Inference Procedure (GRIP) group, subjects received 19 lessons on highlighting key vocabulary terms in texts as clues to making inferences in passages and practiced using the terms to generate their own inferential passages; students and teachers then engaged reciprocally in solving the passages generated. In the basal inference instruction group, subjects received 19 inference lessons taken from 5 third-grade basal reader series. In the control group, subjects continued in the prescribed scope and sequence of the districts adopted basal series. Teachers were trained to teach the lessons in all three groups. The Gates Mac Ginite Reading was used to determine the reading ability blocks. Four comprehensive post-tests were developed for this study; a near transfer test, the inference type test, the close test and the passage (delayed transfer).

The results of the experiment demonstrated that third-grade children can be taught to identify key vocabulary lists and passages to transfer this knowledge to the solution of inference of passages generated and to apply these skills to making inferences in unfamiliar materials.

Levin and Carney (1988) conducted an investigation on "Facilitating vocabulary inferring through root-word instruction." The purpose of the study was to determine whether the manner in which students acquire word components (e.g. ex = out and sect = to cut) affects their ability to infer the meanings of the resulting word composites (e.g. exsect = to cut out). The sample selected for the study was eighty-two undergraduates enrolled in an introductory educational psychology course. Twenty-three of these students constituted a non-instruction control group, and the remaining fifty-nine students were randomly assigned in approximately equal numbers to one of the three conditions in which word components were explicitly taught. The three instructional conditions were — (a) free study which encouraged application of students' own preferred method of study to learn separately 10 word prefixes and 10 stems; (b) semantic — this provided contextual examples that included familiar words containing the prefixes or stems; (c) and mne monic which combined the context examples for learning the prefixes with a mnemonic "Key Word", strategy for learning the stems.

In the semantic condition, prefix learning was done by encouraging students to use a familiar word containing the prefix, along with a sentence example, to help them learn the meaning of the prefix. In the mnemonic condition, the same prefix learning procedure was followed as in the semantic condition. Then for stem learning students were provided with a 'key word' for each stem, which was a familiar concrete word that looked or sounded something like the stem. Each key word was accompanied by a verbally described picture to be imagined, which linked the key word to the stem's meaning. For example, for pel (meaning to push) the key word pill was provided. Subjects were then given the instruction: "Get a picture in your (mind) head of someone refusing to take a medical pill by pushing it off to the side". Three study-test trials were administered.

The criterion test given to all students consisted of two parts. In the first test, subjects recalled the meanings of the components of each compound word. Mnemonic subjects were asked to recall the associated key words also. In the second test which is a multiple choice inference test, subjects were directed to position their root-meanings test right next to the inference test and to use the corresponding root meanings responses to figure out the meanings of the compound words listed.

Following a 3-day interval, subjects returned and were readministered the criterion test of the initial session. Subjects in the non-instruction control condition were given a single test consisting of the 10 prefixes, 10 stems and their compound words. They were asked to supply the meaning of the prefix and the stem (root meaning) and then to answer the multiple choice item pertaining to the compound word (inference).

The test performance results indicated that the subjects in all three instructional conditions had acquired the meanings of prefixes and stems to a high level of mastery (prefix mean = 93 per cent and stem mean 97 per cent). In the control group condition a good many of the component meanings were not well known (prefix mean = 34 per cent and stem mean = 9 per cent). The findings reveal that root word instruction can facilitate the ability of the college students to derive the correct meanings of directly inferable compound vocabulary items. The form in which instruction is delivered does not appear to make a difference.

Porte (1988) analysed "the strategies" adopted by "the poor language learners" while dealing with "new vocabulary". It was done by, conducting interviews with fifteen under-achieving EFL (English as foreign language) learners in private language schools in London. It was found that these learners were using strategies for dealing with new vocabulary which were very similar to those found in studies of 'the good language learner'. They differed in the fact that they demonstrated less sophistication and a less suitable response to a particular activity.

The investigator found that more mature learners who are under-achieving can be encouraged both to identify and appraise their own strategies. For example in a multilingual class where translations are taken from bilingual dictionaries, by comparing the exact meanings in the various mother tongues, attempts can be made to develop a critical awareness of such dictionaries. Activities can be prepared by the class teacher to help weaker learners investigate, step by step their current ways of tackling new vocabulary, comparing their own response at a particular stage of a problem to that of other students. Porte concluded by saying that many poor EFL "learners may often be better served by making sure that we help them to identify, nurture and, where necessary and feasible, refine their own current repertoire of learning strategies".

Palmberg (1988) carried on an investigation on the "computer games and foreign language vocabulary learning". It was an experimental study. Two Swedish speaking boys in Finland aged 9 and 11 participated in the experiment. They both had been exposed to English in the form of television programmes and popular music. The 11 year-old boy had three and half months of English studies at school, two minutes lessons per week. In order to conform to the learners' young age and general interests, a computer adventure game Pirate Cove was used.

The experiment was carried out in three phases. In phase one, the testees were introduced to Pirate Cove and invited to play the game for forty-five minutes, each new word on the screen was provided with an appropriate Swedish equivalent. Phase two was conducted one month later, without prior notice. The time allotted was the same. The programme had not been available to the testees between the two sessions. They were asked to give the Swedish translation for the words displayed. Phase three took place one month after phase two. For this session the testees were given a list of 50 words selected from the target vocabulary. They were asked to give each word on the list a Swedish translation, or that failing to describe any associations triggered off by the words.

The results indicated that in phase one—the testees quickly learned how to read the map and how to navigate on the sea. At the end of the session they also knew how to search specific areas and were able to list what items they had gathered on their journey. They could provide the large majority of the target vocabulary with acceptable Swedish renderings. In phase two, it was evident from the very beginning of the session that the testees had a perfectly adequate working knowledge of the required procedure for playing the game. They were fully in command of how the game options were related to one another, and which actions contributed most efficiently to which sub-goals. As for their vocabulary knowledge, they seemed to have forgotten the dictionary meaning of about half the target vocabulary when asked for a Swedish translation. In the third phase, the testees immediately recognized the vocabulary and managed to assign correct translation equivalent to 35 of the 50 words in the list. Another ten words were attempted although less successfully, whereas five words were left totally unattempted. These findings indicated that computer games, and especially motivating text-adventure games in a foreign language, constitute a good example of material that satisfies the criterion of language needs relevant to young learners of that language, and at the same time promote vocabulary learning.

Computer games can be used as teaching aids in a number of different ways. They can be used primarily on a self-access basis, thus relieving pressure on classroom time and allowing pupils to work at their own pace. Vocabulary learning can be introduced through computer games so as to enhance the vocabulary. The receptive vocabulary activated in the pupils through the games may be reactivated in class and gradually made to become a part of their productive vocabulary.

Shapiro and Gunderson (1988) made "a comparison of vocabulary generated by grade I students in whole language classrooms and Basal Reader Vocabulary". For this study the writings of 52 grade I children in two whole language classroom was collected. The children's writing was transcribed into computer files and the vocabulary was, organised into a rank order list. This list was compared to the vocabulary contained in the Basal Reader Programme used in the school district. The comparison of vocabulary generated by the students with that of the basal readers indicated that high frequency vocabulary was nearly identical. Low frequency words used by students were judged to be more current than those of the basal readers.

The highest frequency word generated by the students is 'and' which was fourth on the Ginn 720 list, while the highest frequency Ginn 720 words is 'the'. The lower frequency words produced by the children contained many more misspellings than high frequency words. However, the correctly spelled words represent wider experiences and are more current than lower frequency words in the basal Readers. This observation reflects not only the children's experiences but also the effects of the thematic approach taken in these classrooms.

The children's draft book writing, as well as their spelling instruction, contained words introduced through other curricular areas. Lower frequency words generated by the children such as 'asteroid', 'disaster', 'astronaut' etc. reflect classroom themes and outside interests, while lower frequency basal words such as bakery, bath, squirrel etc. may not be as relevant to the children. Interestingly many of the lower frequency basal reader words also appeared in the children's writing while the reverse situation was not apparent. A further analysis of spelling errors such as payd (paid) peano (piano) dienosors (dinosaurs) indicate an awareness of sound/symbol relationships. The tendency to overgeneralize their phonic knowledge to irregular words is evident. This overgeneralisation is consistent with a natural development in language acquisition and indicates an awareness of the rule governed systems of language. The results of this study imply that children can develop reading vocabulary as a result of writing activities.

It is concluded that whole language instruction does not limit children's exposure to systematic repetition of important vocabulary. Whole language instruction involves the integration of listening, speaking, reading and writing in a pupil centred classroom setting.

Xiaolong (1988) made a study of "Effects of Contextual cues on Inferring and Remembering Meanings of New Words". The purpose of the study was to find out when verbal contexts can be of significant help (cue adequacy) in vocabulary acquisition and the relationship between inferring and remembering meanings of new words. The study was conducted on second language learners. A sentence with certain input information that contains clues sufficient for inferring the contextual meaning of a target word was defined as a cue-adequate sentence, for example: John took out a collapsible bicycle, unfolded and rode to school. A sentence without input information was defined as a cue—inadequate one, e.g., John took out a collapsible bicycle and rode to school. The subjects for this study were 48 advanced trainees from an EAP (English for Academic Purposes) center in China. They were randomly assigned to four treatment groups, namely, LC– (listening group with inadequate cues); RC– (Reading group with inadequate cues); LC+ (Listening group with adequate cues); RC+ (Reading group with adequate cues). One group i.e., LC– and LC+ took the listening test and the other group, i.e., RC and RC+ took the reading test.

Sixty discrete, semantically disconnected sentences were constructed for the experiment, of which one set were of 30 cue-adequate sentences and the other 30 cue-inadequate sentences. For the listening groups sentences were presented on audio-tapes by means of tape recorders while the reading groups had sentences presented on transparencies by means of overhead projectors, sentenees were shown on the screen. They also had to rate the degrees of difficulty in terms of word inferences, on a nine point scale with '1' indicating the contextual meanings of the 30 target words were 'very difficult' to infer or guess from the sentences the target words were in, '5' indicating 'moderately easy' and '9' very easy. The last task was to test word retention which was done by a cued recall of the target words' inferred contextual meanings.

The results indicated that subjects who received cue-adequate sentences reported greater ease in inferring the meanings of the target words than those who received cue-inadequate sentences. This was true for both reading groups and the listening groups. The subjects receiving cue-adequate sentences scored significantly higher in inferring and remembering the meanings of unfamiliar words in context.

A positive correlation of statistical significance was found between word inference and word retention, further analysis revealed that target words with more powerful retrieval cues were more recallable than those associated with less powerful retrieval cues. This study also revealed that contextual cues being equally adequate, subjects in the reading group scored significantly higher in both word-inference and word-retention than subjects in the listening group.

From the above research findings it was concluded that for second language learners, the text book must be written in such a way that it contains adequate cues in context so as to relieve the learners from the anxiety of unfamiliar words, so that enough information can be created for them to play the 'psycholinguistic guessing game'. Since adequate contextual cues can enhance inferring and remembering the meanings of unfamiliar words in context, 'more comprehensible input' (Krashen, 1983) should be involved in acquiring vocabulary. As reading was found to be more efficient to enlarge their vocabulary, visual patterns of learning should be arranged.

Kern (1989) conducted an investigation into "Second Language Reading Strategy". The purpose of the study was to find out (1) if explicit training in the use of comprehension strategies in second language reading improved the comprehension of students of L_2 texts (2) to find out if explicit training in the use of comprehension strategies in second language and reading improved the skill in inferring the meanings of unfamiliar words in L_2 texts, (3) to find out the word inference ability.

The sample consisted of 53 students enrolled in French. Three at the University of California, Berkeley. In this sample 26 were in the experimental group and 27 were in the control group. Statistics revealed that there were no gross differences between experimental and control subjects in terms of general languages and reading ability in French. The experimental treatment consisted of development in the following areas: word analysis, sentence analysis, discourse analysis, and reading for specific purposes. Subjects were given 'reading task interview' at the beginning and end of the semester in order to assess their ability: (1) to comprehend a French text, (2) to infer the meanings of unfamiliar words from contexts.

In order to investigate the research questions discussed above, a planned analysis using Dunn's method was performed on gain or change scores of the subjects, means and standard deviations of the subject's pre-test, post-test and gainscores on the comprehension measure were calculated. The findings indicated that strategy instruction had a definite positive affect on reader's comprehension of the test passages, subjects who had the greatest difficulty reading L_2 texts appeared to benefit the most from reading strategy instruction. This finding suggests that the middle and high ability readers may have already transferred more of their effective L_1 reading strategies to the second language reading task.

Strategy instruction had a positive effect on subject's ability to infer the meanings of unfamiliar words from context, word recognition and synthesizing meaning in larger segments of text. The findings of this study suggest that it is perhaps better to provide students with systematic procedures for word derivation and contextual inference than to teach long lists of vocabulary items.

Elley (1989) carried out an investigation into the "Vocabulary acquisition from listening to stories". The hypothesis behind this investigation was that children would learn the meanings of many new words that they heard in stories read aloud without explanation of such words, an additional purpose of the study was to attempt to identify word-related and subject-related variables that correlated with vocabulary gain.

The sample consisted of one hundred sixty-eight 7-year old pupils from seven classrooms in seven schools in Christchurch in New Zealand. Each story was read 3 times to the children. The pupil's understanding of the difficult words were assessed through a multiple choice vocabulary test which was pilot tested on 7-and-8-year olds. Half the words were presented as picture vocabulary items, in which the teacher read the word and pupils were to select one of four pictures presented.

Results of the pilot testing showed that several of the target words were widely known by children of this age group. The final test contained 20 words, 10 picture items, 10 verbal synonym items and 4 of the initially selected target words were replaced with synonym. In the final test the story was read 3 times by two different teachers. The results showed that the words that were most readily learned in this story were those for which the surrounding context was helpful, those that occurred more than once in the story, and those that were illustrated in at least one picture. The vocabulary gain was most in the low group. Stories read aloud in this way thus appear to offer a potential source for ready vocabulary acquisition, repeated exposure and helpful context were found to be significant factors in vocabulary acquisition.

As there was no control group, a second study was undertaken by using different books, under different conditions, with a more elaborate design. The purpose of the second investigation was — (1) to confirm the phenomenon of incidental vocabulary learning found in Experiment I, (2) to estimate the effects of teacher explanation of unfamiliar words over and above the effects of reading alone, (3) to clarify further the contribution of word relation and subject related variables investigated in Experiment I, (4) to investigate the permanence of any learning that occurred.

The sample consisted of 127 pupils in two experimental groups, 51 children of similar age and background, as control group. Two contrasting story books were selected for reading. A 36 item multiple choice and vocabulary pretest was used to test knowledge of different words. The test procedure was the same as that of Experiment I. An experimental design was devised to compare the effects of reading the stories aloud with and without explanation of unfamiliar words. The results indicated that the group which heard the story with explanation, had an overall larger gain of vocabulary. The findings from both the experiments support the assumption that young children can learn new vocabulary incidentally from having illustrated story books read to them. Teacher's additional explanation of unknown words as they are encountered can more than double such vocabulary gains.

The studies further revealed that students who start out with less vocabulary gain at least as much from the readings as the other students, and the learning is relatively permanent. It was also found that children will learn a certain word due to the frequency of occurrence of the word in the story, the helpfulness of the context, and the frequency of occurrence of the word in pictorial representation.

Day, Omura and Hiramatsu (1991) carried on an investigation on "Incidental EFL Vocabulary and reading". The purpose of the research was to find out if Japanese EFL students could learn vocabulary incidentally while reading silently for entertainment in the classrooms. The sample selected was two groups of 191 High school and 397 University students. The subjects were given a short story as reading passage with vocabulary items and grammatical structures appropriate for the reading competence, which could be read in 30 minutes by High School students and less than 30 by the University students.

The University students were randomly assigned by class to either a control group or a treatment group, the high school subjects were randomly assigned individually. The treatment group subjects were given the short story for reading. After the story was removed they were given the vocabulary test. The control group were simply given the vocabulary test. The vocabulary test was scored based on the formula: Score: right (wrongs/n-1) where 'n' is the number of choices.

From the results of the vocabulary test it was found that the treatment group subjects scored higher on the vocabulary test. In both groups of subjects those in the treatment group—those who read the story—knew significantly more vocabulary than those subjects (in the control group) who had not read the story. The finding of a casual relationship between reading and indirect vocabulary learning in an EFL context is consistent with research into vocabulary learning by children in their first languages. Like children reading in their first language, the subjects in this investigation attempted to get meaning from the story. This finding that Japanese high school and University students learning English as foreign language can learn vocabulary simply by reading, is of particular importance. One of the curricular implications of this research is that EFL Programmes should include a great deal of extensive reading in order to improve English vocabulary of the students. Hence in the classroom opportunities should be provided for the students to read for pleasure.

Learning of Different Types of Words

Barnard (1961) made "A study of Pre-University (PUC) students vocabulary in Chotanagpur". The sample taken was 750 PUC students in Ranchi University (South Bihar). The test comprised 1600 sentences. The basic item of the test was a structurally simple sentence containing one underlined word for translation into the students' mother tongue. She found that the poorly known words were verbs — 18, nouns — 15, adjectives — 18, and other — 5, out of the average students' recognition vocabulary of 2,100. The conclusions drawn from this study revealed that (i) nouns seemed to be the best known; adjectives were poorly known and logical and temporal connectives and adverbs were unfamiliar, (ii) students were much less familiar with verbs than they were with the vocabulary as a whole.

Chadda (1971) from "A Study of the Vocabulary Resources of Third Year Degree Students" found that the different words known are: nouns 56.6 per cent, adjectives 52 per cent, verbs 50.1 per cent, adverbs 30.7 per cent and others 31.6 per cent. Students failed to distinguish the homonyms like sun-son and their- there, eyes-ice etc.

Agnihotri (1979) carried on an investigation on "Language development among infants in relation to their Social Strata". The findings of the research revealed that the infants of upper middle class used more words, more nouns, adjectives, adverbs, verbs and longer sentences. Girls used more nouns, adjectives and adverbs, but so far as the pronouns and verbs were concerned, there was no difference in their language.

Kumar (1982) after the "Assessment of entering behaviour in English of pupils of Standard VII" reported that the pupils were very low in the use of five component skills, viz., the use of phrases, prepositions, degrees of comparison, and plurals. The proficiency of the pupils in the use of articles, opposites, and the -ing forms was average.

Rao (1982) from his study "A diagnostic study of Reading disability among school children" reported that the students performed fairly well on the subtest in word meaning in antonyms, but were poor and below average achievers in the subtests of word meaning with prefixes and suffixes and word meaning with their roots.

Nation and Liu Na (1985) from their study on "Factors affecting guessing vocabulary in context" found that verbs are the easiest to guess, nouns are next, then adverbs and finally adjectives.

Schwartz (1988) carried out an investigation on "Early action word acquisition in normal and language impaired children". In this study the acquisition of words referring to three types of actions was examined in normally developing and language impaired children whose speech was limited to single word utterances. They served as subjects.

The children were presented with 12 experimental words in 5 sessions over a period of approximately 3 weeks. The experimental words referred to actions that were classified as intransitive, transitive and specific to a particular object, or transitive but performed on four different objects. The children in both groups produced few of the action words. The groups differed in their comprehension of the three action word types. The language impaired children did not exhibit differences in comprehension across the different types of actions. The language—normal children comprehended fewer words for intransitive actions than for other types. Children in the early stages favour object words over action words.

Elley (1989) after his study on "Vocabulary acquisition from stories" reported that children achieved the highest gains on nouns, and less improvement on adjectives and verbs, when they heard stories with explanation. From reading without explanation, the children improved by an average of 24.2 per cent on nouns from either book, whereas on the adjectives and verbs they showed a mean gain of only 5.9 per cent on the nouns like 'roadster', 'pizzazz' and 'never-do-well' they showed mean gains of more than 30 per cent whereas on the adjectives and verbs 'rote', 'strewn' and 'melancholy' they showed no gain at all.

Organisation of Language Text Book—Vocabulary Acquisition

Barnard (1961) made a study of Pre-University (PUC) students vocabulary in Chotanagpur of Ranchi University in south Bihar. While investigating into the acquisition of the vocabulary of PUC students, the researcher made a study of the text-book and found that there was very little grading of vocabulary in the text-books and even when it was graded it was not selectively presented and taught, or repeated enough to establish it. The new and old words occurred with random density. The text material itself was insufficient in quantity. It was also found that the students were much influenced by Indian English and as such she suggested that Indian English should be brought into the school texts instead of the elaborate literary language.

Olson (1965) conducted an analysis of the vocabulary of Seven Primary Reading Series. The study aimed to find out the following facts — (a) the number of words introduced (vocabulary load) (b) whether there was a smooth and progressive increase in the introduction of the new vocabulary within each series from one level to the next (c) whether there was any difference in the development of the vocabulary from one series to the next (d) whether there was a core vocabulary same as the Dolch Basic Sight vocabulary of 220 service words.

Seven Primary Reading series were taken as the sample. In this study the author checked for the cumulative number of words appearing at each level of the series, and the number of new words introduced at each level. It was found that all the Basal Readers did not introduce new words at the same rate nor do they have the same vocabulary load. Regarding smooth transition of vocabulary from one level to the next, it was found that there is a percentage increase in the number of new words introduced at each level. Maximum increase in the introduction of new words was noticed at the primer level. The minimum percentage increase of the new words was 58.38 per cent and the high increase was 87.61 per cent. The percentage increase at the pre-primer one and two level is not very significant. There was an enormous increase in the number of new words introduced as the student progressed from the third pre-primer of all the series in the primer level.

There was only minimal agreement between words common to five or more of the series studied. The development of the vocabulary load varies from series to series with a noticeable increase from the third pre-primer to the primer level. The diversity of words in the series lead to the conclusion that the teacher would no longer rely on a basic core vocabulary list to help her give the students the vocabulary background that would enable them to go from one series to another with ease.

Nair (1975) conducted "A study of the concept of standards in English through an Analysis in the text-books prepared for Secondary school pupils in Kerala". The objectives of the study were to analyse the text-books in English prescribed for study for the secondary school pupils in Kerala since 1952 and to compare the findings, and to find out the concept of standards in English. The procedure followed were—setting up tentative criteria for arriving at the concept of standards in English, qualitative and quantitative analysis of the text-books, and a study of the concept of standards of attainment and achievement. The findings revealed that the density indices of vocabulary were the highest for standard VIII, the lowest for standard X and fluctuating in Standard IX.

The early readers contained a large number of difficult words and archaisms. The index of new words in the text-books was satisfactory but the spacing and repetition of new words was not satisfactory. The structural words were the items of most frequent occurrence in the books. Vocabulary was a neglected item in the text books, especially in the early years.

Marzano (1984) conducted a study to identify a number of vocabulary clusters. According to Mezynski (1983) there are four positions regarding vocabulary instruction, namely (1) the aptitude Position, (2) the access Position, (3) the instrumental Position and (4) the knowledge Position. The aptitude position attributes vocabulary development to inborn characteristics that are relatively unaffected by instruction. The access position considers vocabulary ability as an amalgam of trainable subskills. Proponents of this position are interested in automatically believing that a vocabulary item becomes truly usable only when the student can recognise and understand it immediately. The instructional implication is that practice and time spent on developing vocabulary are the key.

The instrumental position states that vocabulary determines how the reader processes information, so if vocabulary knowledge is the entry point, teaching it systematically should be an educational priority. The knowledge position asserts that knowing a single word implies knowing a lot of related words in large chunks of information. A new word is probably entered into an individuals store of concepts by attaching it to appropriate clusters of concepts. The instructional implication is that vocabulary words should be taught along with the semantic clusters to which they belong.

It is believed that there might be a small number of clusters or chunks of concepts that account for most of the words commonly used in English. If these basic clusters could be identified, they might be a powerful instructional tool. In the light of the utility of vocabulary, the author made an effort to identify the vocabulary clusters. The investigator selected a corpus of 7,230 words from the Basic Elementary Reading Vocabulary (Harris and Jacobson, 1972), supplemented by the word Frequency Book (Carroll, Davies, and Richman, 1971) and the word Frequencies of spoken American English (Dahl, 1979).

The investigator categorized these words into semantically related groups or clusters using the rule of thumb "what grouping would be most applicable in a class-room?" The concept clusters were given to 60 elementary schools teachers for review and to identify if any word did not fit well in an instructional sense. All identified words were reclassified. This step was repeated until less than 5 words in 1,000 were identified as miscategorized by the participating elementary school teachers.

Through the above process the investigator produced three levels of clusters: Superclusters, Clusters, and

Miniclusters. Superclusters, are the largest organizational chunks: There are 61 of these broad semantic categories. Clusters are groups of words with closer semantic ties than superclusters: There are 430 clusters. The miniclusters are those which have the strongest semantic ties: There are over 1,500 of these. A few of the examples of constituent words in the superclusters identified by Marzano are as follows:

1. Occupations: Career, manager, mayor, coach, businessman, printer, publisher.
2. Type of motion: Action, stillness, begin, end, chase, toss, pull, plunge, shrink.
3. Size/quantity: Tiny, large, amount, many, monstrous, one, two.

It was found that the first 15 superclusters accounted for over 50 per cent of the vocabulary students encountered in written materials in grades K-6, the first 25 superclusters accounted for over 70 per cent. He suggested that the superclusters could form, the skeleton for vocabulary instruction, and perhaps be the core of a spiral curriculum. He further tested these superclusters on small groups of children and found that highly significant gains in concept knowledge, vocabulary knowledge and reading comprehension were achieved using a systematic cluster approach.

Konopak (1988) conducted a study on "Eighth Grader's Vocabulary learning from inconsiderate and considerate text". This study examined differences in eighth grader's vocabulary learning from two versions of contextual information in two history text passages. The major purpose of this study was to determine if content text could be rewritten such that students' comprehension of unfamiliar topic words could be enhanced. Specifically, keeping content constant, eighth grade state history text selections were presented to high and average ability eighth graders in one of two versions: (a) an original version in which inconsiderate text factors would prevent reasonably complete, accurate word learning, or (b) a rewritten version in which the contextual information was made more considerate by adhering to the aspects of completeness, explicitness, proximity and clarity of connection.

Subjects selected were 55 eighth grade students enrolled in two state history classes at a university laboratory school. They were stratified by reading ability according to their reading percentile scores on a standardized achievement test and then grouped by high and average ability levels.

Instructional materials for this study included two passages extracted from an eighth grade state history text (Davis, 1976). With the assistance of an eighth grade History teacher, the researcher identified 15 content words per passage, each meeting the following criteria: (a) it was specific to the topic, (b) knowledge of its meaning would aid in topic understanding, (c) a precise meaning within the history context would likely be unknown to the subjects. This selection resulted in words of middle to high level of importance in the passages, which while not necessarily crucial for general comprehension, would increase in-depth understanding of the topic.

From these lists, 10 target words then were chosen as being embedded in inconsiderate text. Contextual information in each original passage was rewritten according to the four text features to be more considerate for each of the 10 target words per passage, this revision was at sentence level only. Thus, the instructional materials included an original version and a revised version of the two text passages. All target words were underlined each time they appeared in text to focus the subjects attention.

The pretest consisted of the 20 target words (10 per passage—two passages) listed in isolation by random assignment. Each word was followed by spaces labeled "yes", "some", "no", and "meaning". The study was conducted on three separate days. On the first day pretest was conducted in which, the students were asked to mark "yes", if they thought they knew the word reasonable well, to check "some", if they had partial knowledge of the word or to check "no", if they did not know it. The succeeding two days involved text reading (original and revised version) and post-testing. Suitable statistical techniques were applied to the obtained pre-test and post-test scores.

The results showed that the revised text passages elicited greater learning for all students than did the original text passages, suggesting that the four text characteristics, namely, completeness, explicitness, proximity and clarity of connection, were of some value in making text considerate for word comprehension. This is an important finding considering that eighth-grade students are expected to become independent learners and as a consequence may depend on the subject text for word learning.

Two educational implications suggested are: first text-book publishers need to be aware of the concept and nature of inconsiderate text for word learning and the relatively simple revision procedure to make text considerate. Second, content teachers must also be aware of the limitations of contextual information in terms of their students' acquisition of partial/erroneous knowledge, and be prepared to support vocabulary development with instruction.

Wodinsky and Nation (1988) studied about "Learning from Graded Readers". In this investigation a word frequency study was made of two graded Readers and an unsimplified text to determine the contribution that Graded Readers can make to vocabulary learning. While analysing the text-books it was found that in order to master the vocabulary at a particular level, it would be necessary to read several texts at that level. It was also found that when moving from one level to another it is not necessary to learn the vocabulary of the previous levels in order to read successfully at the new level. Two simplified reading books were selected for this study. One was called "An Indonesian Love Story" and was written at level four in the Longman Structural Reader Series. Level four consists of a vocabulary

1,100 words. The other text was "White Mountains", which was written at the same level in the same series. While analysing the two texts by taking frequency counts. It was found that the longer the text the more likely most of the vocabulary will be repeated.

A large number of words in the Graded Readers were repeated often enough to ensure their being learned. Graded Readers were obviously found to allow learners to do large quantities of reading within a limited vocabulary. Graded Readers provide much more favourable conditions for reading and vocabulary learning than unsimplified texts do. In order to meet the vocabulary used in graded readers enough times ensure learning, it would be necessary to read several readers written at the same level. This study has looked at the possibility of learning and coping with vocabulary in graded readers. The major factor looked at here is repetition.

Thames and Readence (1988) conducted a study on "Effect of Differential Vocabulary Instruction and Lesson frameworks on the reading comprehension of Primary children". This study compared the use of vocabulary instruction in a traditional basal reader format with that of two other lesson frameworks: (a) Reconciled Reading Lesson (RRL) and (b) List Group Level (LGL) as a means for improving comprehension of basal stories.

The sample for this study consisted of 75 second graders from a public school located in moderate sized Southern city. These students were placed in their respective classrooms by homogenous grouping procedures. Testing and grouping assignments were conducted by the various classroom teachers and administrators in the school system. Subjects participating in this study were randomly assigned to one of three instructional groups, traditional basal lesson, RRL, or LGL.

The instructional material selected was G 900 reading series, each one had to read 3 story selections which were selected by a panel of five judges with experience in using basal readers with primary level children. They are: (a) Morris has a cold, (b) Pea soup and Sea Serpents and (c) Feather in the wind. The traditional basal reader format involved writing the pre-selected vocabulary words on the board and having the subjects select an appropriate sentence in which to use them. The RRL followed a general format adapted from Reutzel (1985) and included instruction in the same vocabulary words pre-selected by the basal series. In this RRL approach more attention is focussed on background information at the beginning of the lesson sequence prior to having the children read a basal selection. The students are given a broader range of opportunities to incorporate as well as expand and enrich their background knowledge. This approach is termed by Reutzel (1985) as Reconciled Reading Lesson (RRL). As a pre-reading activity, the RRL seemingly requires students to become active as well as effective users of story concepts and their appropriate terminology. It is believed that such an activity might help students resolve the conflict prior to reading and allow for maximum comprehension.

The use of List Group Label (Taba, 1967) is similar to semantic mapping, it provides such an instructional format to the students. In this strategy students are asked to brainstorm and think of words or expressions related to stimulus words that have been taken from the text. In this way students are assisted in activating and organising their prior knowledge about a text. Through evaluation of selected words and student input teachers are given the opportunity to expand and/or alter students, prior knowledge of a topic using repeated vocabulary so that it accurately fits the material to be read. An instructional strategy like LGL focuses on the notion that not only can students' vocabulary be broadened, but also through oral discussion each individual student can be given a broader view of the concept in question. Pre-test was conducted to find out the prior vocabulary knowledge of the students in the three stories. In the post-test there were 10 vocabulary and 10 comprehension questions. Items were assessed by a panel of judges for clarity, content and passage dependency.

The results of this investigation showed that the post-test vocabulary scores accounted for 46 per cent of the variance in comprehension scores of the students. This indicates that vocabulary knowledge played a substantial part in the outcome on the comprehension post-test measure. It was found that RRL did enhance the ability of the subjects to understand the basal stories. Based on the findings of the study the implications suggested by Dana and Readence (1988) are that RRL appears to be a strategy that teachers might consider using, the teachers ought to reconsider the importance of vocabulary instruction and pre-teach those words which will help students understand the concepts present in the basal stories.

Influence of Social-Psychological Factors on Acquisition of Language Skills

Lambert and Gardner (1959) investigated into the "Motivational variables in second-language learning". They administered a number of attitudinal and motivational variables to a group of 11 students studying French in Montreal. A factor analysis of the relationships among measures of language aptitude, attitudinal and motivational characteristics and teacher ratings of students' proficiency in French resulted in the extraction of four factors. One of these factors was defined primarily by the indices of language aptitude, thus supporting the conclusion that achievement in French was related to individual differences in language aptitude.

The second factor was attitudes towards French Canadians, motivational intensity to learn French, and integrative orientation towards language study, indicating that achievement in a second language was associated with a willingness or desire to learn the language of a valued second language community for the purpose of communicating with them. These two factors namely language aptitude and attitudinal characteristics were orthogonal to each other suggesting that achievement in a second language was related to these two independent components.

After one year Gardener (1960) repeated this study but included more indices of attitudinal/motivational characteristics and a greater sampling of second language skills. He confirmed the results obtained in 1959. He showed that Montreal-English speaking were apparently reflecting their parents' attitudes to French speakers.

Wilbur (1964) had undertaken a study of the "Understanding Vocabulary of First Grade Pupils". The purpose of the study was to construct and validate a test to measure the estimated size of the basic English Understanding Vocabulary of grade one pupils. The proposed test was based on a word sample of five hundred words selected at random from Funk-Wagnalls New Standard Dictionary, 1952 edition.

The five hundred words were subjected to a process of elimination first by the researcher, then by College graduate students and finally ten sixth graders, and there remained 121 words. The multiple choice test items were constructed. The test was administered to 272 first grade pupils in fourteen different classrooms and ten communities in the State of Maine. The California Test of Mental Maturity, Primary Edition, results were secured for all pupils. The reliability and validity of the test were established, and the reliability was found to be 0.79 indicating that the test was a consistent instrument.

Correlation coefficients were computed to determine the relationship of intelligence and understanding vocabulary size. A correlation coefficient of 0.49 was found between intelligence quotients and the understanding vocabulary test scores of the 272 first grade children which indicated that there was a relationship between vocabulary and intelligence. No significant differences were found in the size of basic understanding vocabulary of Grade One boys and girls. The "Z" ratio of 0.25 in favour of the girls was not significant.

Carroll (1967) conducted a study on "Foreign language proficiency levels attained by language majors near graduation from College". Based on the findings he has suggested that the attitude of parents matters much. He found that "The greater the parents use the foreign language in the home, the higher were the mean scores of the students. Thus, one reason why some students reach high levels of attainment in a foreign language is that they have home environments that are favourable to this, either because the students are better motivated to learning, or because they have better opportunities to learn" (Carrolla, 1967: p. 138).

A study was undertaken by George and Visweswaran (1967) about the acquisition of vocabulary in English upto the end of standard V. The purpose of the study was to bring out the common errors committed by pupils when they used selected vocabulary in writing, the facilities in teaching and learning vocabulary in schools and connected studies over factors such as social, educational, sex, locality, management type of schools and medium of instruction.

The sample consisted of 228 boys and 98 girls among which 117 were from Tamil medium and 209 were from English medium schools, 140 were from upper primary schools and 186 were from secondary schools, 169 represented the rural area and 15 urban area, 170 were from schools of public management and 156 were from aided schools. The sample was a stratified random one.

The test results showed that there was no significant difference between boys and girls in their acquisition of English vocabulary. Pupils who studied in English medium schools were found to be superior to that of the Tamil medium students. Pupils of the upper primary section of the secondary schools were superior to the pupils in the upper primary classes in senior basic schools. Pupils studying in private management schools scored more in vocabulary than the pupils studying in public management schools. Pupils of urban schools achieved more in vocabulary than the pupils from rural schools. The analysis of the questionnaire revealed that teachers were the easiest source of help in learning English, majority of the pupils (68.38 per cent) liked their English teachers very much, nearly half of the sample selected for the study (47 per cent) liked more to speak in English rather than to read, write or listen. It was found that more than half of them (57.7 per cent) spoke more to teachers than to parents or friends.

The investigators had brought to light several factors which had a direct relationship with pupils' acquisition of English vocabulary. The factors were — (1) interest in learning English, (2) liking of the subject, (3) linking of the English teacher. They also found that there was significant correlation among factors such as pupils health, power of hearing, power of sight etc. and the acquisition of English vocabulary. The study also found that the there was high relationship between the stability of the pupils emotions and English vocabulary.

Spolsky (1969) carried out an investigation on "Attitudinal Aspects of Second Language Learning". According to him attitude is the fourth factor that has been proposed to account for variation in the level of achievement in the second language acquisition. In a typical language learning situation, there are a number of people whose attitudes to each other can be significant: the learner, the teacher, the learner's peers and parents and the speakers of the language. Each relationship might well be shown to be a factor controlling the learner's motivation to acquire the language. In this study the author was concerned with finding out more about integrative motivation by developing an instrument that would compare a subject's attitude to speakers of a foreign language in which he already has some degree of proficiency.

The sample consisted of 79 students in group I who had arrived in USA to attend American Universities, 71 similar students in Group II who were attending a seminar at the University of Minnesota, 135 foreign students in Group III enrolled for the first time at Indiana University and 30 Japanese students in Group IV who were students of Indiana University. The proficiency of the students in the sample was studied in relation to their attitude towards the speakers of the language. This study reaffirmed the importance of attitude as one of the factors explaining the degree of proficiency the student achieves in learning a second language. It was found that a person learns a language better when he wants to be a member of the group speaking the language. Learning a second language is a key to possible membership of a secondary society: the desire to join that group is a major factor in language learning.

Koppar (1970) conducted "An Enquiry into Factors Affecting Reading Comprehension" (in English). The purpose of the study was (i) to find out the level of Reading Comprehension of Standard XI students of Gujarati medium, (ii) to find the relationship of Reading comprehension with attitude towards reading, anxiety academic motivation, SES and dependence. The sample consisted of 555 students of XI class from 9 Gujarati Medium Schools of Baroda.

The tools used in the study were: The silent Reading Comprehension Test in English for SSC constructed by Patel, the reading attitude scale of Patel, Junior Index of Motivation Scale of Frymier, Test anxiety Scale for Children constructed by Nijhawan, the SES scale constructed by Mehta and pre-adolescent Dependence Scale developed by Parekh and Rao. Descriptive statistics and product moment correlation were used for data analysis.

The major findings of the study were: Reading comprehension was related positively to Reading attitude.

Some other factors related to Reading Comprehension were found to be (a) reading readiness, (b) academic motivation, (c) attitude towards the study of English, (d) quality of classroom teaching, (e) presence or absence of proper direction, (f) educational level of parents, (g) social and economic compulsions.

Chadda (1971) conducted an investigation into the Vocabulary Resources of Third Year Degree Students. The purpose of the study was to compile lists of essential words which constitute the vocabulary for comprehension purpose at degree level, to assess the range of recognition vocabulary of an average degree student, to make observations about the part played by the level of education of parents, medium of instruction at school, performance at examination and the age at which the study of English was started.

The sample selected was 110 students of 3 colleges in Osmania University. She found that there was correlation between performance of students at the PUC public exam and vocabulary test. The investigation showed that the educational background of the students' parents does not have any bearing on their score of vocabulary test in second language. Reading habits of students and their attitudes towards English affect vocabulary. Students who read books, magazines and newspapers fared better on the test.

Pillai (1973) has done a study on "The Effect of Social and Psychological Factors on Achievement in English". The investigator has studied the effect of sociological factors on the three languages, namely, Malayalam, English, and Hindi. The study was conducted on 694 subjects of which 347 were boys and 347 were girls. The sample consisted of pupils of IX class selected on stratified random basis from ten secondary schools of Trivandrum, Palghat and Khozikode districts of Kerala. In the selection of the sample, factors such as sex, rural-urban, locale of the pupils and school efficiency were considered.

The tools used were the composite test of generalized achievement standardized by Nair, Abraham and Seethamani for measuring achievement in English and

Hindi; and for Malayalam the Kerala University Generalized Test of Achievement in Malayalam standardized by Nair and Ero; the Socio-Economic Status scale developed by Nair consisting of items on order of birth, family size, educational level of father, vocational level of father, income level of father (and SES of pupils). Pearson's 'r' was used to find the relationships between the achievement in language and each of the select sociological factors.

The results indicated that the six sociological factors did influence the achievement in languages. Educational level of father, vocational level, income level and SES of father were found to be significant factors contributing to high achievement in English. But it was found that the higher the order of birth, and size of the family, the lower the achievement in English. Regarding achievement in English and Hindi though the influence of home ground is felt, other factors such as intelligence are more significant.

Jordan (1978) conducted a five year perspective study of child development to find the "Influence on Vocabulary Attainment". He found that the following important aspects influence the vocabulary attainment: how parents encourage the child's vocabulary through conversation, word games, reading to the child, providing reading materials at home and indicating to the child, that learning in general and word knowledge in particular are valued.

Gardner, Smythe and Clement (1979) investigated the relationship between French achievement (language) and a series of attitudinal/motivational variables. The sample for the investigation consisted of 89 Canadian and 65 American adults students in an intensive French language programme. The purpose of the study was to assess the effects of the programme on attitudes, motivation and French proficiency. The results demonstrated an association between an attitudinal/motivational factor, referred to as integrative motive, and French oral proficiency and reported satisfaction with the programme for the sample of 89 Canadian students, but not for the 65 Americans, even though an integrative motive factor was obtained with both the samples. Results were interpreted as reflecting the role played by attitudes in the language learning situation, but attention was directed toward the significant influences the socio-cultural background of the student can have on the nature of this role.

Shaw (1979) made a survey of the attitude of the students towards English and reported the results in the "English and the Indian Student". The sample consisted of 342 final year degree college students from 6 colleges in Hyderabad, Andhra Pradesh. The study was conducted with the assistance of CIEFL (Central Institute of English and Foreign Languages) and the cultural learning institute of the East-West Centre. The instrument used was an English language questionnaire. The collected data dealt with five major topics: (1) the English background of the respondents, (2) the pattern of their present and future use of English, (3) their reasons for studying English, (4) the English skills they desired and (5) their general attitude towards English.

The results of the survey indicated that their future use of English would increase. Given a list of 25 possible reasons for studying English, the three groups, namely, English major, engineering and commerce, when asked to indicate the extent to which those reasons were representative of their own feelings, unanimously picked up the following two common reasons:

(a) I studied English because I will need it for my work. English 93/4, Engineering 95/3, Commerce 94/4.

(b) I studied English primarily because it is required in our system.

English 85/10, Engineering 78/16, Commerce 79/10.

The other reasons received positive ratings by all the groups. Most of the reasons are those which are usually mentioned as indicators of an integrative type of motivation stemming from a desire to join or be like a group of native speakers. It showed that English is mainly studied for instrumental purposes.

The respondents were asked to indicate their degree of agreement or disagreement with a number of statements representative of certain attitudes towards English. This was to discover more about their personal feelings towards the English language. The response to such statements illustrated a number of points like: Although the status of English as a compulsory subject was often cited as a major reason for studying it, a majority of the students in each field felt that they would try to learn English even if it were not a required subject. It appeared that most of them had very positive attitude towards the language.

Shah (1979) conducted "A comparative study of some personal and psychological variables and Reading Comprehension". The main objectives of the study were to compare intragroup differences in subject scores on Trivedi and Patel's Reading Comprehension Test with respect to six personal variables viz., sex, grade, age, parental income, parental education and parent occupation as well as three psychological variables viz., reading rate, intelligence and meaning vocabulary. The sample consisted of 412 pupils of 8th and 9th grades drawn from four different secondary schools of Bhavanagar city.

The results indicated that there was significant difference between 2 grades as well as medium age groups. There was significant difference in frequencies of high and low group pupils on the variables of parental income, parental education and parental occupation. There were significant differences in frequencies of 3 different groups of pupils on all the three psychological variables, namely, reading rate, intelligence and meaning vocabulary. Correlation values of the last three variables with reading comprehension indicated positive relationship between them.

Agnihotri (1979) carried on an investigation on "Language development among infants in relation to their social strata". The objectives of the investigation were (1) to study the language of infants aged four to five years, (2) to study the factors which affected language development, namely, SES, sex and birth order, and (3) to study certain peculiarities of language development such as context of words, specific expression, use of spoken form, local dialects etc.

A sample of 36 infants stratified on the variables of mental age, social class, sex and birth order was selected, through the incident sampling procedure. The tools administered were SES scale developed by Jalota, Pandey, Kapoor and Singh, and eight stimulating pictures developed by the researcher with the help of some judges. The findings of the investigation were—the infants of upper class and upper-middle used more specific expressions and context free expressions than the infants of middle class, there was significant difference in the language of boys and girls, there was no difference in language of infants of different birth orders.

Lasman, Fisch et al. (1980) after the study of "Early correlates of Speech, Language and Hearing" reported that individual differences in vocabulary are related to socio-economic variables such as parental income, occupation and education.

Bhishikar (1980) while investigating on "An Experimental Analytical study of the Acquisition of Reading Skill" also worked on vocabulary. One of the major objectives of the investigation was to prepare a training programme in reading skill containing exercises for comprehension, vocabulary, mechanical perception and reading speed with accuracy. The findings of the investigation revealed that intelligence played a significant role in the acquisition of reading skills, the high intelligence group showed significantly greater improvement in vocabulary; SES, reading habit, reading interests, health, language and scholastic achievement were found to be significantly related to reading achievements.

Patrikar (1981) carried on an investigation on "A linguistic analysis of the errors in written English of students of B.A. Classes of the colleges in urban centres of Vidarba". The study was concerned with the causes of deterioration in the usage of English and it was analysed by critical examination of errors in language performance of students in the university examinations. The investigation was limited to written expression in English. In all 1500 written-valued answer books of candidates from Nagpur, Akola and Amarnath were collected. In addition 400 scripts from colleges in these cities were also obtained. Out of 1900 scripts, 300 were sorted out after careful scrutiny. One hundred sentences from these scripts were examined for description and explanation of the errors committed in each category such as (i) omission of lexical items, (ii) orthographical, (iii) morphological errors, (iv) syntactical errors. The study revealed that the student's knowledge of English vocabulary, morphology and syntax was very confused. The reasons for the major deficient achievement is attributed to psychological and environmental causes.

Kumar (1982) made an assessment of "entering behaviour in English of pupils of standard VIII". The main objectives of the study were to assess the attainment in the different component skills of written English of a representative sample of 600 pupils of standard VIII, selected from Trivandrum district in Kerala. It included 300 urban and 300 rural pupils and 279 boys and 321 girls. The tools used were word fluency test, free composition of about fifteen sentences and entering behaviours English test specially prepared for this study which included ten component skills of written English. After the administration of the tools and data analysis it was found that the vocabulary attainment of standard VIII pupils was very low, boys and urban pupils were found to have significantly higher attainment than girls and rural pupils respectively. On the four types of errors boys and urban pupils had significantly lower number of incorrect responses.

Subramanyam (1981) conducted an investigation on "some correlates of Reading Achievement of Primary School Children. The aim of study was (i) to develop a reading achievement test in Telugu (language) for the use of Primary School Children, (ii) to establish norms for vocabulary and paragraph comprehension, (iii) to compare the sex-wise reading preference of students in urban and rural areas, (iv) to establish the relationships of reading achievement of children with their personal characteristics, school conditions, home background and socio-economic factors of the family, (v) to identify the contributing factors to reading.

The sample consisted of 1200 pupils studying classes III to VII an the Primary, Upper Primary and Secondary schools of Andhra Pradesh. Stratified random sampling procedure was followed. The tools used were: (i) a specially designed reading achievement test in Telugu to measure the vocabulary and comprehension level of the pupils, (ii) Raven's Progressive Matrices Test to measure the non-verbal intelligence and (iii) questionnaire to collect information on personal, social and psychological aspects. The major findings of this study were Reading achievement was comparatively low in rural areas. Personal characteristics, namely, age, intelligence, general health, vision, speech, reading habits and mother tongue had positive influence on reading achievement whereas sex of the child showed no such influence. Reading facilities provided at home, time spent on reading activities at home, and parental help and encouragement had significant relationship with reading achievement.

The caste group, educational level and income of the family showed a positive influence on children's reading achievement, but the occupation of the parents, social participation of the members of the family and types of family they belonged to had no such relationship. Home environment played a prominent role in reading comprehension of children and the reading achievement of children in socially and culturally backward areas was very low.

Rao (1982) conducted an investigation on the Reading disability among school children. The main objectives of the study were (i) to investigate the main causes of reading difficulties, (ii) to identify and analyse the psychological, sociological, and educational factors affecting growth in reading performance, (iii) to relate reading difficulties with achievement in certain school subjects, (iv) to make case studies of school children with special type of reading difficulties. A sample of 300 students studying in class V, VI and VII of ten schools in Andhra Pradesh were selected following stratified random sampling procedure. Due representation was given to the sex of the individual, location and management of the school. After the application of suitable statistical techniques to the data obtained from reading test and questionnaire items, it was found that there was high correlation between vocabulary and comprehension and also between reading skills and language achievement (0.64).

Among the personal characteristics studied, visual discrimination, auditory discrimination, general health condition and general mental ability of the children showed high positive relationship, reading skills of children were most dependent on the socio-cultural background of their families. Students from highly developed and culturally advantaged families fared better on reading tests when compared to those children who hailed from backward and culturally disadvantaged families. Children from socially and culturally backward families suffered from language deficiency and lagged behind in the reading skills.

Khanna and Agnihotri (1982) investigated into "Language Achievement and some social psychological variables". The purpose of the present research was to investigate the comparative significance of some social psychological variables in second language achievement. In a pilot study, the achievement in English of twenty Hindi speaking first year undergraduates of the University of Delhi was seen in relation to nineteen social psychological variables, e.g. attitude towards English, exposure to English, family background, motivation, authoritarianism, ethnocentricism etc. The language achievement was assessed by a battery of tests on skills such as Vocabulary, grammar, reading comprehension and writing. For listening comprehension, the students were asked to answer multiple type questions after listening to a tape-recorded lecture of a university teacher.

Proficiency in oral skills was tested through individual interviews and the recorded interviews were evaluated on five components of oral skills, viz., pronunciation, grammer, vocabulary, fluency and comprehension on a five point scale. The study examined the relationship of six achievement variables with nineteen social psychological variables. A correlation matrix for these 25 variables was obtained. The results indicated that achievement in English is effectively predicted by such social psychological variables as proficiency in English medium of instruction, exposure to English through novels and films, use of English at home, previous scores in English, non-ethnocentricism, and democratic feelings towards others, positive attitude towards other languages and mother's education. The above generalisations were drawn from the pilot study. The same set of tests were administered to a large sample of 86 informants, and the results analysed, did not show any significant deviations from the major findings reported in the pilot study.

Tejovathi (1988) studied about the "Environmental Factors Affecting the Acquisition of the English Skills". The purpose of the study was to find the relationship between the English language skills and the overall environment which included the linguistic, home, social and cultural environments. The study also attempted to know the effects of the three variables i.e., locality, sex and SES (Socio-Economic Status) of the family on the acquisition of English language skills, the effect of the locality, sex and SES on the listening performance and reading attainment in English; and the performance of students in two components i.e., word comprehension and general comprehension selected for the study.

The study was conducted on a sample of 660 students of IX class—boys and girls of rural and urban locale. The tools consisted of open-ended opinionnaire to the teachers, questionnaire and listening and reading comprehension tests to the students.

The research findings showed that the environment factors had a positive effect on the acquisition of English language skills. The linguistic, home, social and cultural factors also had a positive influence on the English achievement of the students; the urban environment was found to be better than rural in all the factors; the sex of the child did not affect the performance in English. The effect of locality and SES was more on listening comprehension than on reading; no difference was found between the students performance in word comprehension and general comprehension.

INFERENCES

From the review presented, it is clear that different methods are in use to develop the vocabulary skills among the children of different grades. However the translation method is widely used in Indian classrooms and the teachers made use of Indian English. In some of the experimental studies it was found that the bilingual method was superior to the direct method in developing the language skills; definition + context was found to be better than the definition presentation in the acquisition of vocabulary; vocabulary presentation through reading stories aloud to children was found to be acting positively in the pupils' acquisition of vocabulary; computer games were found to help students learn vocabulary in an informal way and so on.

In learning types of words, different researchers found that nouns seemed to be best known; adjectives were poorly known and logical and temporal connectives and adverbs were unfamiliar. In some other studies it was found that students performed fairly well in word meaning in antonyms, but were poor and below average in word meaning with prefixes and suffixes.

With regard to the organisation of the text-books it was reported by the earlier researchers that there was very little grading of vocabulary in the text-books; the basal readers did not introduce new words; the density indices of vocabulary were the highest for VIII grade and lowest for X grade; the longer the passage, the more frequent would be the occurrence of new words; contextual presentation and words presented in known situations were helpful; cluster approach would help students increase their vocabulary; considerate text-book was found to contain contextual information; when words are repeated it would ensure vocabulary learning; List Group Label was found to contain instructional format etc.

From the study of the influence of different variables on vocabulary acquisition and language skills studied, it was identified that age, attitude, motivation, intelligence, emotional stability, general health, interest, medium of instruction, SES, etc. had positive impact on language skills; sex difference exhibited bipolar results—in some studies no difference between boys and girls was identified in acquiring language skills (Wilbur, 1964; Subramanyam, 1981; George and Visweswaran, 1967); in some other studies boys proved superior to girls (Agnihotri, 1979 and Kumar, 1982). With regard to birth order no difference was found by Agnihotri (1979) and higher the birth order lower was the English achievement (Pillai, 1973). It was reported by some authors that there was no influence of parents educational background on the acquisition of English vocabulary of their wards (Chadda, 1971) and positive impact was reported by Koppar (1970), Pillai (1973) and Shah (1979).

Thus the researches carried out in this area had mostly adapted either survey method or experimental method. The survey method was used to study the acquisition of different types of vocabulary, vocabulary presentation in the text-books and the influence of different variables on language skills and the experimental method was used to find out the effectiveness of different methods of teaching vocabulary.

In the light of the above inferences and observations, the problem for the present investigation is stated with its objectives, hypotheses and variables that are to be studied in the following chapters.

3

Statement of the Problem, Hypotheses and Variables

Man is a social being. Man lives in the society. In the society he needs to communicate. The communication be it oral or written is done through language. Language is an essential tool for man. Language is made up of words. Words are the symbols for the ideas and experiences. The stock of words or the vocabulary that man possesses gives him confidence to communicate effectively. Man starts accumulating these words from the time he is born into this world.

As a child, one picks up the words that are uttered into his ear. Just as food is essential for the physical growth and development of the individual, there is need for the intake of the vocabulary into the mind for the mental growth and development, which would enable him to master the language. A large vocabulary is essential for mastering of a language. With limited vocabulary the learner is in danger of collapsing due to misunderstanding. If too many words are misunderstood, the learner hardly knows where to start. Learners find it exceedingly difficult to fight their way into rapid conversation where words so easily collide with one another. Knowledge of words is hence very essential. Lack of English vocabulary is a major problem for second language learners.

Extensive research has been done on the study of vocabulary acquisition of English as a first language in various parts of the world. Research in English vocabulary acquisition in India is scanty. Hence the present study has been undertaken by the investigator.

Statement of the Problem

In the light of the review of related literature, the title of the present investigation is stated as follows: "A study of the acquisition of active and passive vocabulary in English of students of X class in relation to certain social and psychological factors". The study is proposed to examine the differences in the vocabulary acquisition of boys and girls residing in the urban and rural areas. It establishes the relationship between vocabulary acquisition and some other variables namely students mental ability, socio-economic status, educational level of the family, general health, (students' reported impression of their visual and auditory acuity), classroom teaching, attitude towards English text and English class, home environment, leisure time activities and psychological factors (students' expressed fears related to English language).

Objectives of the Study

The study is undertaken with the following objectives:

(a) To find out the acquisition of English vocabulary of X class pupils.

(b) To compare the acquisition of English vocabulary of students in rural and urban areas and among boys and girls.

(c) To establish the relationships between acquisition of English vocabulary (of X class students) and other variables namely mental ability, socio-economic status, educational level of family, general health, classroom teaching, their attitude towards English text-books and English class, home environment, leisure time activities and psychological factors.

HYPOTHESES

According to Goode and Halt (1952) 'a hypothesis states what we are looking for. It is a proposition which can be put to test to determine its validity. It may prove to be correct or incorrect'. There are four types of hypotheses.

They are:

(a) Questionnaire form,

(b) Declarative Statement form,

(c) Directional Statement form and

(d) Null form.

The Null hypothesis assumes that observed difference is attributable by sampling error and true difference is zero. The statistical test of significance is used to accept or reject the Null hypothesis. For the present study the investigator formulated the Null hypotheses to test the statement of the problem. The Null hypotheses for this study was stated as follows:

1. There would be no sex differences in the acquisition of English vocabulary of the X class students.
2. There would be no urban and rural differences in the acquisition of English vocabulary of X class students.

   (a) There would be no difference between urban boys and rural boys in the acquisition of English vocabulary.

   (b) There would be no difference between the urban girls and rural girls in the acquisition of English vocabulary.

   (c) There would be no difference between the urban boys and urban girls in their English vocabulary acquisition.

(*d*) There would be no difference between the rural girls and rural boys in the acquisition of English vocabulary.

3. There would be no sex and locale differences in the performance of the X class students in different sections of the vocabulary test.

   (*a*) There would be no difference between the boys and girls, urban and rural students in their performance of the test items—identifying meaning.

   (*b*) There would be no difference in the performance of the different variables in the question on identification of the problem word from the clues given in the context. All are the same in their performance.

   (*c*) There would be no difference in the performance of the different categories of students in the item on completion. All are the same in doing that part of the test.

4. There would be no relationship between the acquisition of English vocabulary and non verbal mental ability of the X class students.

5. There would be no relationship between the acquisition of English vocabulary and the socio-economic status of the X class students.

6. There would be no relationship between the acquisition of English vocabulary and the educational level of the family.

7. There would be no relationship between the acquisition of English vocabulary and the general health of the X class students.

8. There would be no relationship between the acquisition of English vocabulary and the attitude towards English of the X class students.

9. There would be no relationship between the acquisition of English vocabulary and the classroom teaching activities of the X class students.
10. There would be no relationship between the acquisition of English vocabulary and home environment of the X class students.
11. There would be no relationship between the acquisition of English vocabulary and their leisure time activities.
12. There would be no relationship between the acquisition of English vocabulary and the psychological factors of X class students.

VARIABLES

It is obvious that the dependent variable in this investigation was vocabulary acquisition of the X class students.

Although there are different independent and intervening variables which may influence the dependent variable, a few of such variables were considered in this study. To be more specific the independent variables included in this study were non-verbal mental ability, socio-economic status, educational level, general health (students' reported impressions of their visual and auditory acuity), attitude towards English text and class, classroom teaching, home environment, leisure time activities, and psychological factors (students' expressed fears related to English language).

The two personal and demographic variables namely, sex and locality (rural and urban) were also considered in this study. A brief description of the variables studied in the investigation is as follows:

(i) *Vocabulary Acquisition:* It is the power of the student to recognise and recall the meanings, synonyms, antonyms, usage and other forms

of the words selected from the English Reader of IX class in use during 1984-89. Here vocabulary is inclusive of both active and passive vocabulary because all the 395 words in the text-book are tested only at the recognition level. The correct responses of the student in the vocabulary test was considered as vocabulary score of the student.

(ii) *Mental Ability:* The performance of the students on the non-verbal mental ability test of Raven's Progressive Matrices is taken as the mental ability.

(iii) *Socio-economic Status:* The data about the occupation of parents, income, type of house in which they live, land owned, the vehicles in the house and other goods such as fridge, television, radio, fan etc., was collected to place them in high, middle and low, SES groups.

(iv) *Educational Level of the Family:* In this study Education refers to the formal instruction undergone in school or college to get a certificate for the successful completion of the course. The appropriate weightages are given to college, high school and elementary school education to obtain a single score which refers to the educational level of the family.

(v) General Health (students' reported impressions of visual and auditory acuity and speaking skills): In this study the term general health refers to the physical well-being of the children. Those children without any impediments of vision, hearing and speech were considered to have good health. Information about continuous absence of the pupil from school due to prolonged sickness like typhoid or malaria, was collected to decide about the general health of the pupil.

(vi) *Attitude:* It is the mental stance of the student with regard to English. Some students had positive attitude, this was decided on the basis of their liking to learn English words, English reader, English class etc. It is considered that this liking or disliking influences the learning of the 'subject.

(vii) *Classroom Teaching:* In this study classroom teaching refers to the formal instruction the teacher gives to make the students understand the meaning and usage of new words in English.

(viii) *Home Environment:* Environment refers to the physical and social conditions in which the children live. In this study the meaning is restricted to the conditions that promote the learning of English. In some homes the parents speak to their children in English, they encourage children to speak in English or participate in activities that would promote the learning of English words. Where a child got maximum encouragement it was considered to be a very conducive home; no encouragement an unconducive home and minimum encouragement a conducive home.

(ix) *Leisure Time Activities:* Activities which the children do for interest or pleasure during their free time are referred to as leisure time activities. For this investigation, study of free time activities was limited to such activities as reading English stories, books, cartoons, viewing TV, listening to radio talks in English etc.

(x) *Psychological Factors:* Anxiety, fear, boredom, worry, excitement about English class and learning English words is considered as psychological factors in this study.

4

Methods of Investigation

This chapter describes different methods employed in carrying out the investigation. The first part of the chapter deals with measurement of variables—both dependent and independent variables—and the development and adaptation of the tools used to measure the variables. In the second part of the chapter the research design, the methods employed in the selection of the sample, collection of the data, scoring the responses of the subjects and analysis of the data are described.

MEASUREMENT OF THE VARIABLES

The dependent variable of this investigation is the vocabulary acquisition of the X class students. To measure this variable, a vocabulary test was developed. To measure the independent variables viz., mental ability, socio-economic status, educational level of the family, general health of the students etc., two instruments were used. They are: (i) Raven's Progressive Matrices (Black and White) to measure the non-verbal mental ability of the student, (ii) a questionnaire consisting of personal data of the students and their perceptions about — (a) socio-economic status, (b) educational level of the family, (c) general health (Students' Reported Impressions of their Visual and Auditory Acuity and Speaking Skills), (d) attitude towards English, (e) classroom teaching, (f) leisure time activities, (g) home encouragement, (h) psychological factors (students' expressed fears related to English language) to obtain the data about all other independent variables. The adaptation and construction of the above tools are described in the following pages.

CONSTRUCTION OF THE VOCABULARY TEST

The aim of the present study was to find the acquisition of English vocabulary in relation to certain social and psychological factors. Several studies on vocabulary have shown that a vocabulary test is used to measure vocabulary and a questionnaire to collect information about the related factors.

The test was designed to be one of recognition type consisting of eleven sections, Shastri (1972) had also used recognition type test items.

The vocabulary test was constructed based on the list of words that the X class students had studied in their previous year of study i.e., in their IX class. Harris (1969) in his book on Testing English as a second language says that for the vocabulary test, the words can be taken directly from the text-books that have been used in the class. Kaushik (1974) had constructed a vocabulary test based on the IV, V and VI class books in Hindi for his investigation on Basic Hindi vocabulary. Some others who had followed similar procedure in the construction of test items from the class books are Shukla (1976), Bhal (1975) etc.

After a study of the previous literature it was considered appropriate to measure the dependent variable namely English vocabulary by constructing test items to elicit response for the knowledge of the word meaning, judgement in choosing the most appropriate word in a given contextual situation (Jennifer Sullivan—Sociolinguistic Review of the Iowa Tests of Basic Skills) the knowledge of antonyms and synonyms, prefixes and suffixes in word formation (Lado, 1970; Harris, 1969). Several writers of books on language testing argue that sentences can more easily provide effective context clues than phrases. Hence the investigator presented most of these items in contextual situation. When separate measurement is given to vocabulary, largely, it is through the device of a guided response test. The test items were thus constructed with reasonable contextual clues as suggested by Bradfield (1957) in Measurement and Evaluation in Education.

Planning for the Test

The IX class reader was studied to plan for the vocabulary test. The tool was prepared in the year 1985-86.

The prescribed IX class reader at the time of testing the X class students was prepared by Sasikumar of Central Institute of English and Foreign Languages (CIEFL) Hyderabad and was published by the Government of Andhra Pradesh. The same book was in use upto 1989-90. The new book was introduced in June 1990.

The IX class reader contained 395 new words. All the words were taken into consideration for the construction of test items. As the number of words is quite large, the vocabulary test was split into smaller tests according to the unit in which they were introduced. When the number of words was less than fifty in any unit it was combined with another unit.

After a study of the literature available on language testing by various authors such as Lado (1970), Harris (1969), Valette (1977), Heaton (1983), Richards (1976) etc., test items were prepared for all the words introduced in the IX class Reader. The list of words given in the Appendix of the Reader and the words listed as new words in each unit were underlined in the Reading passage in order to know in what sense the word was used. Care was taken to see that the test item contained the same contextual meaning as given in the reading passage. Some vocabulary which could be covered under opposites and other word families like the formation of new words with prefixes and suffixes were tested for the same. The list of words distributed in the different units is shown in Table 4.1.

Table 4.1: Distribution of Words in Each Unit

Unit No.	*Name of the lesson*	*Number of Words*	
		Active Vocabulary	*Passive Vocabulary*
1.	A Great Social Worker	56	4
2.	I Met A Bushman	26	4
3.	The Wrong House	47	2
4.	Albert Einstein	54	5
5.	The Apple Tree Complex	35	–
6.	The Wrong Spring	6	7
7.	My Wild Dog Booto	46	4
8.	The Thief's Story	50	5
9.	The Lap of Honour	39	5
	TOTAL	359	36

Bradfield (1957) says that multiple choice items with 3, 4, 5 or 6 possible answers from which the testee is asked to choose, are more difficult to construct and less economical of space. Their chance factor is less than that of true/false and they can be keyed to more complex elements of knowledge. Wilbur (1964), George and Visveswaran (1967) etc., made use of the multiple choice test items. For the present study the multiple choice test items were constructed in view of the advantages of such a type of test items. All the test items were of multiple choice. Although the total number of words were 395, the total number of items were only 371 as the matching type of multiple choice items consisted of four words each. The different types of items used in the present study are shown in Table 4.2.

From the table 4.2 it is known that more test items were given in Meaning identification, One word for many and completion, the least number of items were of Meaning from context. The different types of test items were selected on the basis of the literature on language testing. The types of items used were as follows:

Table 4.2: Unitwise and Typewise Distribution of Test Items

Sl. No.	*Type of Test Item*	*Unit*									*Total*
		1	*2*	*3*	*4*	*5*	*6*	*7*	*8*	*9*	
1.	Meaning Identification	12	6	10	11	8	3	10	11	7	78
2.	One word for many	12	6	10	11	7	2	10	11	8	77
3.	Completion	15	6	9	11	7	2	10	11	9	80
4.	Definition	5	5	5	4	2	1	5	3	3	33
5.	Word Associations	7	-	4	4	1	3	9	2	2	32
6.	Antonyms	5	3	2	6	3	-	-	3	-	22
7.	Prefixes	-	-	-	-	4	2	2	3	8	19
8.	Suffixes	-	-	6	5	-	-	-	6	1	18
9.	Meaning from context	-	-	-	-	1	1	-	1	1	4
10.	Matching	1	1	1	1	1	-	1	1	1	8
	Total No. of Items	57	27	47	53	34	14	47	52	40	371

1. **Meaning Identification:** One method of testing vocabulary is to underline a word in context and provide several possible meanings (Harris, 1969). It has been experimentally proved that providing context very markedly improved the test results. Words tested in context are more meaningful than the words tested in isolation.

It can quite effectively measure understanding of lexical items because the "problem word appears in context". According to Heaton (1983) "vocabulary is much more usefully tested in context since it is the context that gives specific meaning and relevance to a word, thus creating a situation which is as linguistically valid as possible in the circumstances". The same items were used by Harris (1969) and Chadda (1971). The present investigation consisted of 78 test items of this type in the pilot study. Example from Harris:

John was astonished to hear her answer.

A. greatly amused B. greatly relieved C. greatly surprised D. greatly angered.

Example from the present investigation:

Radha was popular in the class.

A. liked by many B. deceived by many C. hated by few D. loved and hated.

2. **One word for many:** A variation of the above test. In this type the problem sentence remains the same but the examinees are asked to substitute one word for the underlined portion. It is slightly modified from the one given in the book of Harris (1969). In his book the student has to rewrite the whole sentence substituting other words. But in the present investigation, the student has to identify one word that can be substituted for the group of words. Vocabulary items of this type are relatively easy to construct and they effectively measure

understanding of lexical items. In the pilot study there were seventy-seven items of this type. This was also given by Valette (1977) and Heaton (1983).

Example from Harris:

1. John was greatly surprised to hear her answer.

   A. John was amazed to hear her answer.

   B. John was astonished to hear her answer.

Example from present study:

He played this tune over and over again.

A. rarely B. horribly C. repeatedly D. sweetly

3. **Completion:** This type of item places the problem word in context. This type of item has the advantage of placing the problem word in the context setting, a procedure felt by many to provide a better measure of candidates' ability actually to use the test words actively in a real life situation. Moreover it allows the testing of many words which cannot be briefly defined (Harris, 1969). In certain ways the items shown in this section are more difficult to construct than those in the previous section. It is mainly because of the context: too little context is insufficient to establish any meaningful situation, while too much context will provide too many clues (both grammatical and semantic). For many such items the context itself provides grammatical clues which automatically rule out at least one of the options. This type of test items were also found in "Teaching and Testing of Vocabulary Items" by Shabbir Ahmed (1972), Valette (1977), Harris (1969), Heaton (1983) etc. Eighty test items of this type were included in the pilot form.

Example from Harris:

The old woman was too __________ to push open the heavy door.

A. feeble B. sincere C. deaf D. harsh

Example from the present study:

Padma tied rakhi around the__________ of her brother.

A. finger B. arm C. palm D. wrist

4. **Definition:** This type of item is described by Harris (1969) as a classic type of vocabulary item. In this type the test word is followed by several possible definitions or synonyms. A variation of this type places the definition first and the problem word in the multiple choice. The students are asked to select the word that corresponds to a target language. This type was found in Teaching and Testing of Vocabulary Items by Shabbir Ahmed (1972), Harris (1969) and Heaton (1983). Thirty-five test items were set for the pilot study.

Example from Harris:

A brief, light sleep.

A. nap B. yawn C. stroll D. hug.

Example from the present study:

Something wrong with the body, a weak leg, hand, blind, deaf, dumb etc.

A. handicap B. ugly C. handsome D. charmless

5. **Word Association:** This is a type of item which is given out of context. In this type the students are asked to associate pairs of words. Many of the difficulties arising from the testing of collocations are avoided by the testing of word sets. In such tests the students familiarity with a range of associations is measured. Classification type of item was also included in this type. Valette (1977), Heaton (1983) have described this item. The number of items given in this was thirty.

Example from Valette:

Match the words that go together.

1. Pilot

A. Hospital 2. Doctor B. Courtroom C. Aeroplane Select the appropriate category

Scarlet: A. Colour B. A day of the week

C. An item of clothing D. A song bird

Example from the present study:

Temperature: A. Colour B. Sea C. Heat D. Nature

6. **Antonyms:** This type of item was also given out of context. The students had to indicate words closest to meaning the opposite of the word given in capital letters. This type of item was used in UPSC (Union Public Service Commission) examination, and it was there in Valette (1977) too. Some words are learnt better when paired with its antonym. Twenty-three items were given in pilot study. When a preliminary study was conducted on a hundred students in order to find out the suitability of the various items, the antonym type was given at the production level. The students were asked to complete the opposite word for the underlined word by giving the first and last letter as clues. The students expressed great difficulty in doing it and so this was avoided in the pilot study.

Example from Valette:

Jean begins his work.

A. does not organize

B. wants to stop

C. finishes

D. is hungry during (C)

Example from the present study;

WAR A. Peace B. Fight C. Piece D. Destruction

7. **Prefixes:** A variation of the antonyms given above is to select the prefix that would form the opposite of the word. This type of item was found in Heaton (1983) and the class text-book. Twelve items were given in this category. Similar items were given for words which were not opposites.

Example from Heaton:

(IM) possible ( ) important

Example from the present study:

_______possible A. in B. no C. mis D. im

Go forward: _______ceed A. suc B. pre C. pro D. ex

8. **Suffixes:** Pupils learn to recognize related words and form more words based on the principle of word families. Vocabulary items of this type can assess the ability of the student to produce related forms. This item was slightly modified from the one given in Modern Language Testing—Valette (1977). The word in its incomplete form was given in the sentence and the pupils had to identify the most suitable suffix that could be added to it.

Example from Valette:

Give the related nouns:

Stupid Answer: Stupidity.

Example from the present study:

The teacher lost confid ______ in the mischievous boys.

A. ence B. ance C. erate D. ment

Bundle packed together: pack - - - - ( )

A. ize B. age C. able D. ory

9. **Meaning from Context:** Knowing a word means knowing many of the different meanings of the word. The meaning of the word depends on the thought that it is being used to express and the context of its expression. A very large number of words in a dictionary have multiple meanings. The word takes its meaning from the context in which it is used. In the Reader there are some words with two meanings, presented in two different units. The word is used with one meaning in one unit and a different meaning in another unit. The examples given in the Reader are as follows:.

If winter comes, can spring be far behind.

I put the wrong spring in the machine.

kind — A. type B. helpful

present — A. here, now B. a gift C. not absent

This type of item was suggested in "The Role of Vocabulary Teaching" by Richards (1976). Four items of this type were given in the pilot study.

Example from Richards:

Scan means to glance at quickly and to read in detail. Example from the present study.

There is a spring in some pens.

A. leap B. season C. coil of metal D. jump

10. **Matching:** A new type of matching item was adopted from the candidates Manual for the UPSC examination. The students have to match the words in list A with the meanings given in list B, and select the correct answer using the code given for it. Four choices are given in the code. In a matching item of this type, the possibility of getting the correct answer by a simple process of elimination can be avoided. As this was not a familiar type of matching item, it was explained. Care was taken to see that the pupils followed the procedure of working out the answer. Four words were given under this item but the answer was scored as one. Altogether eight sets of matchings were written for the pilot study.

Example from the present study

A		B		Code
1.	Vast	a.	see	A - 1 2 3
2.	Raise	b.	large	c a d
3.	Look after	c.	lift	B - 1 2 3
		d.	care for	b c d
				C - 1 2 3
				d c a
				D - 1 2 3
Answer (B)				b c a

Pilot Study

The test items prepared for measuring the acquisition of English vocabulary were first given to experienced school teachers, lecturers in colleges of education, and experts in the field of education, for correction. Their suggestions and corrections were taken into consideration and necessary changes were made in the test items. The pilot test was administered to a sample of 370 students studying X class. It would be convenient to have 370 subjects in the sample of pilot study for carrying on item analysis by considering top 27 per cent (N_t=100) and bottom 27 per cent (N_b=100) of the subjects as criterion groups (Kelley, 1939). The sample included both boys and girls from urban and rural locale. As the test was long with 371 test items for 395 words, it was divided into smaller tests according to the units. The investigator personally visited six schools about six times each to administer the tests. The list of schools where the pilot study was conducted is given in Table 4.3.

Table 4.3: List of Schools Selected for Pilot Study

S.No.	*Name of the school*	*Locale*
1.	Bandlamudi Hanumayamma Girls High School, Guntur.	Urban
2.	Lutheran Model High School, Guntur.	Urban
3.	Sri Majety Guravaiah High School, Guntur.	Urban
4.	Sri Jalagam Rama Rao Municipal High School, Guntur.	Urban
5.	St. Ann's Girls High School, Phirangipuram.	Rural
6.	Z.P. High School, Angalakunduru.	Rural

Scoring and Item Analysis Procedure

The answer papers collected after administering the tests were valued with the help of the scoring key. The marks secured by each candidate in all the tests was found by adding up all the test scores obtained by each subject. The answer scripts were then arranged in the ascending order. The top 27 per cent (100) and the bottom 27 per cent (100) scripts were analysed itemwise.

The correct response to each test item by the top 100 and the bottom 100 was counted separately as PH and PL. PH stands for percentage of the subjects who answered correctly in the high group and PL stands for the similar percentage in the low group. The PH and PL scores were tabulated, and discrimination and difficulty values were calculated.

Item Difficulty Level

The difficulty level of a test item provides some indication of the extent to which the item is doing its job. The power to differentiate between the students at various achievement levels is necessary if the test is to have adequate construct validity. An item which everyone passes does not provide such differentiation, nor does an item which everyone fails. An item in which 90 per cent of the criterion groups answered correctly would be considered as an easy item. One which only 10 per cent answered would be termed as very difficult. An item that half of the criterion groups answered correctly and the remaining half answered incorrectly is said to have 50 per cent difficulty. The difficulty of an item is indicated by the total number of subjects who answered it correctly, the larger this number the easier the item.

Facility index is a term used by the British. The American term used for the same is referred to as the difficulty index. A measure of the difficulty level or facility index may be obtained on the basis of the item data for the combined high and low groups. The difficulty index is computed by dividing the number of pupils passing the item by the total number of pupils in the combined high and low groups; the value thus obtained is multiplied with 100. In the present investigation the number of subjects in the high and low groups was 100, hence the calculation can be further simplified as follows:

$$\frac{P_H + P_L}{100 + 100} \times 100 = \frac{P_H + P_L}{200} \times 100 = \frac{P_H + P_L}{2}$$

$$FI = \frac{\text{No. right High PLUS No. of Right low}}{\text{Total No. in High PLUS Low groups}} \times 100$$

FI: Facility Index

(Harper and Harper, 1990, p. 358)

Ph = Percentage of passes in the high group

Pl = Percentage of passes in the low group

Diederich (1964) recommends that FI should always be rounded off to the whole digits. According to him recording an FI as "56.36" is silly.

Item Discrimination

A measure of discriminatory power may also be obtained on the basis of the high and low groups. The basic function of all educational measurement is to place individuals along a defined scale in accordance with differences in their achievement. Such a function implies high discriminative power on the part of the test. Since tests are made up of separate items, each item comprising a test must have this quality in a maximum degree if the total test is to possess it. Discriminative power in a test or a test item means that a different quality or magnitude of response may be expected from individuals or groups possessing the abilities in question in varying degree. Pupils with superior ability should answer the item correctly more often than should inferior pupils. The purpose of the Discrimination Index (DI) is to find out whether or not the item is measuring the same ability as the test measures. It is a measure of the correlation (relationship) between the item and the total test score. Its calculation is very simple. It is done by subtracting for each item, the number in the Low group from the number in the High group who answered it right and dividing this difference by the maximum possible difference between the two groups (i.e., by the total number in one of the extreme groups, either high or low). The formula for calculating the DI is as follows:

$$DI = \frac{\text{No. right High MINUS No. right Low}}{\text{No. in EITHER high OR low group}} = \frac{P_H - P_L}{100}$$

(Harper and Harper, 1990, p. 360)

Selection of Test Items for the Final Test

The total number of test items constructed for 395 words were 371 as the test item of the matching type consisting of four words was counted as one item. The items with the discrimination index of 0.35 and above and the difficulty value between 25 per cent and 75 per cent were selected for the final form of the vocabulary test. The final test was printed. The list of the selected items is shown in Table 4.4. The total number of items selected for 164 words was 152 for the final study.

As seen from the Table 4.4 words from all the IX units were selected for the final test. The words include both passive and active vocabulary. No distinction was shown in the construction of test items for the active and passive vocabulary. Of the 36 words given under passive vocabulary, 8 words were selected and out of the 359 active vocabulary, 156 words (150 items) were included in the final test.

Reliability

To quote from Garrett (1985, p. 337) "A test score is called reliable when we have reasons for believing the score

Table 4.4: Distribution of Items Selected for Final Test

Description	Unit									Total
	1	2	3	4	5	6	7	8	9	
Meaning identification	3	2	4	8	2	-	4	2	1	26
One word for many	6	2	6	9	4	-	4	4	3	38
Completion	12	4	7	8	2	-	2	5	3	43
Definition	5	1	3	-	1	1	2	-	-	13
Word Associations	5	-	4	1	1	1	4	-	2	18
Antonyms	3	1	-	1	-	-	-	1	-	6
Prefixes	-	-	-	-	-	1	-	-	2	3
Suffixes	-	-	2	3	-	-	-	2	1	8
Meaning from context	-	-	-	-	-	1	-	-	-	1
Matching	-	1	1	-	-	-	-	-	-	2
Total	34	11	27	30	10	4	16	14	12	158

to be stable and trustworthy. Stability and trustworthiness depend upon the degree to which the score is an index of "true ability" — is free of chance error". The correlation of the test with itself is called the reliability coefficient of the test.

There are four methods of determining reliability, viz., 1. Test-retest (repetition) 2. Alternate or parallel forms 3. Split-half technique 4. Rational equivalence.

In the test-retest method the same test is repeated on the same group and correlation is computed between the first and second set of scores. If the test is repeated after a very short interval, many subjects may recall their first answers and spend time on new material and thus tend to increase their scores, it may have the memory effect. If the second administration is done after sufficient interval, memory practice and other carry over effects may be reduced. Then the retest coefficient becomes a close estimate of the stability of the test scores.

When alternate or parallel forms of a test can be constructed, the correlation between the two forms—A and B may be taken as a measure of self correlation of the test. This method is satisfactory when the two forms are developed with equal difficulty and discrimination value (of all the items). This procedure has two advantages viz., (1) one need not be concerned about memory and practice effect, since the two forms of the test are composed of different items, (2) a more accurate estimate of reliability is likely to be obtained because the estimate is based on a larger sampling of the universe of test items. "The estimate of reliability obtained in this way is often called a coefficient of equivalence and stability" says Lindeman (1971, p. 46). It is more difficult to construct two forms of a test than to construct just one and in addition there are problems of ensuring that the forms are indeed equivalent.

In the split-half method, the test is divided into two equivalent halves, and the correlation found for these half-tests. Two sets of scores are made up by combining alternative items in the test. The first set of scores represents performance on the odd numbered items 1, 3, 5, 7 etc., and the second set of scores performance on the even numbered items 2, 4, 6 etc. From the self correlation of the half-tests, the reliability coefficient of the whole test may be estimated from the formula:

$$r_{11} = \frac{2r_{\frac{I}{2}\frac{I}{II}}}{1 + r_{\frac{I}{2}\frac{I}{II}}}$$

(Spearman Brown prophecy formula for estimating reliability from two comparable halves of a test)

Where r_{11} = reliability coefficient of the whole test and

$r_{\frac{I}{2}\frac{I}{II}}$ = reliability coefficient of the half-test, found

experimentally (Garrett, 1985, p. 339).

The method of rational equivalence represents an attempt to get an estimate of the reliability of a test free from the objections raised against the other methods given above in this procedure two forms of a test are defined as 'equivalent' when corresponding items a, A, b, B, etc., are interchangable and when the inter-correlations are the same for both forms. The formula used is as follows:

$$r_{11} = \frac{n}{(n-1)} \times \frac{\sigma^2 t - \Sigma pq}{(\sigma^2 t)}$$

(reliability coefficient of a test in terms of the difficulty and the inter-correlations of test items)

in which

r_{11} = reliability coefficient of the whole test

n = number of items in the test

σ t = the SD of the test scores

p = the proportion of the group answering a test item correctly

q = (1 – p) = the proportion of the group answering a test item incorrectly (Garrett, 1985, p. 341)

The present study made use of split-half method to find the reliability of the test. The value was found to be 0.82. Hence the test is a reliable one.

Validity

The validity of a test is the extent to which it measures what it is supposed to measure and nothing else. Every test, whether it be a short informal classroom test or a public examination should be as valid as the constructor can make it. The most common types of validity relevant to an achievement test are face validity, content validity and construct validity.

A superficial inspection of the test items would reveal whether the test is valid or not. This type of validity is referred to as face validity: If a test item looks right to other testers, teachers, moderators and testees it can be described as having face validity. In the present investigation the vocabulary test was shown to English lecturers in College of Education, School teachers teaching the particular class and it was even given to the pupils as a try out and necessary changes were made, based on their suggestions. Hence the test has face validity.

The content validity depends on a careful analysis of the language being tested and of the particular course objectives. From the content area the test items can be prepared, there are two aspects in this part, viz., content relevance and content coverage. In the present study the vocabulary listed in the class text-book as new words was taken and for the content coverage test items for all the new words in all the units were constructed. Hence the vocabulary test is said to possess the content validity.

A test has construct validity if it is capable of measuring certain specific characteristics in accordance with a theory of language behaviour and learning. This type of validity assumes the existence of certain learning theories or constructs underlying the acquisitions of abilities and skills. For example if the assumption is held that systematic language habits are best acquired by means of the structural grammar approach, then a test which emphasises the lexical or situational meaning of language (rather than the structural meaning) will have low construct validity.

In the present investigation the test items were designed to test the vocabulary acquisition of the pupils. The test items were constructed in such a way that the lexical meaning was emphasised. The subjects ability to identify the meaning of the lexical items, to identify the right usage of the words, to locate the opposite words and to form new words by adding prefixes and suffixes was tested. Hence the vocabulary test may be said to possess construct validity.

CONSTRUCTION OF QUESTIONNAIRE

The aim of this study was to find the relationship between the acquisition of English vocabulary and other social and psychological factors. A questionnaire was constructed to measure the social and psychological factors. The different factors studied were grouped under the headings of:

(a) Socio-Economic Status

(b) Educational Level

(c) General Health

(d) Attitude of the pupil towards English Classroom

(e) Classroom instruction regarding English Vocabulary

(f) Home Environment

(g) Leisure Time Activities

(h) Psychological Factors

(i) Mental Ability

(a) ***The Socio-Economic Status*** (SES) scale used by Subramanyam (1981) and Tejovathi (1988) was adopted for the study of the SES. The information regarding parents occupation, income by way of salary and other means, the kind of house they lived in, the agricultural land owned, vehicles and other luxury goods possessed was taken into consideration to place the subjects in the different socio-economic status position.

(b) ***Educational Level:*** The educational level of all the members in the family was collected with the help of a table prepared carefully by the investigator. The same procedure was followed by Subramanyam (1981) in his study on "Some correlates of Reading".

(c) ***General Health*** (Students' Reported Impressions of Their Visual and Auditory Acuity and Speaking Skills): The information regarding the overall health of the pupil was drawn through the statements. Subramanyam (1981) had made use of 17 items to collect information about visual ability, good health, hearing and speech habits. But the present investigation used only 4 items to collect information about visual ability and one for hearing and one for health. George and Visveswaran (1967) had followed the same procedure.

(d) ***Attitude:*** The statements organised under classroom activities contained 10 items related to the attitude of the pupil towards reading English, liking or disliking the English subject, the English Reader etc. The statements were given under five point scale—with the markings on — Always, Frequently, Occasionally, Seldom and Never. George and Visveswaran (1967) also used this type of tool.

(e) ***Classroom Instruction:*** The information about how the teacher introduced the new words and what audio-visual aids vere used was elicited from the pupils. The pupils had to record their perceptions about the teaching of English. The statements were given under the five point scale. The sum total of all the statements was taken into consideration for deciding about good classroom instruction, average and poor. Similar information was collected by George and Visveswaran (1967) in their investigation.

(f) ***Home Environment:*** Some parents encourage their children in learning English words, they speak to them in English and also encourage them to participate in activities that would increase their contact with English language and thus help to increase their vocabulary. This information was elicited by framing related statements on five point scale. Answers to these statements were classified for analysis as indicating much, some or no parental assistance in learning vocabulary as classified by Morris (1967).

(g) ***Leisure Time Activities:*** Information regarding the pupils out of school activities that would help in the acquisition of English vocabulary was elicited through a number of statements given under five point scale. This part of the questionnaire was written based on the study of Morris (1967). Information was collected on television viewing, radio listening, reading English story books, comics, doing English word puzzles, riddles, writing to or getting letters in English from pen friends etc. The information thus collected was classified for analysis as favourable, and not favourable leisure time activities with some in between.

(h) ***Psychological Factors*** (Students' expressed fears related to English language): Statements about the pupils fear, anxiety, inhibition, emotional imbalance etc., were placed under psychological factors. Krashen (1979) in Language Teaching Methodology argues that learning caused by fear and anxiety is lowered. He further says that "an activity is good for second language acquisition if it provides. . . . low anxiety situation". The statements were given under five point scale, and the sum of weightages on all the items was considered as desirable psychological factors, medium and undesirable for analysis.

Scoring—Questionnaire

The responses to the questionnaire were given suitable weightages to obtain the sub-total scores on each one of the variables included in the questionnaire. Except on the first three variables the items were given weightages as in the case of Likert type of items.

Validity and Reliability

The questionnaire with all the details was submitted to a panel of judges consisting of experts in the field of education, lecturers in colleges of education, experienced teachers etc. for their comments. Their suggestions were incorporated in the final version of the questionnaire. Thus the instrument is said to possess content validity.

The instrument was administered to 100 tenth class student consisting of both boys and girls from rural and urban schools. The questionnaire was readministered on the same sample of students after 15 days. The two sets of scores obtained by the sample were correlated. The range of the correlation coefficients for all eight parts of the questionnaire was 0.53 to 0.87. Thus the test retest reliability coefficient was found to be significant on all the parts of the questionnaire.

A Brief Description and Adoption of RPM

Vocabulary acquisition of the pupils was studied in relation to their non-verbal mental ability. The non-verbal mental ability was measured by Raven's Progressive Matrices (RPM) by adopting the tool. RPM is preferred to other verbal intelligence test as the latter correlate very highly with the dependent variable, i.e., the vocabulary test. By adopting RPM it would be possible to measure components other than verbal ability in the intelligence.

The matrices consist of five sets A, B, C, D and E. Under each set there were 12 figures making a total of sixty figures. Each figure varied from the other in its composition or design. Each set was in the increasing order of difficulty. The subjects had to record their responses in a separate sheet given to them.

The selected sub-sample of subjects were administered the RPM test. While administering the test necessary instructions were given in detail and care was taken to avoid any form of copying. At any point of time not more than 25 children were administered the test. The time taken by the subjects ranged from 30 to 45 minutes. The subjects showed keen interest in doing the test. Each one of the children was supplied with a booklet and also a response sheet. Before the commencement of the test an example of answering an item was demonstrated to them. They were also instructed how they have to record their responses in the response sheet.

Thus to measure the vocabulary acquisition, a vocabulary test, to measure the non-verbal mental ability the RPM and to record the perception of the students on different social and psychological factors, a questionnaire was prepared for the purpose of data collection.

The Research Design—Survey Method

The aim of the present study was to find out the English vocabulary acquired by the pupils studying X class and the factors associated with the acquisition. After a careful study of the previous literature the investigator selected the survey method and testing procedure to get answers to the problem about vocabulary acquisition. In the survey method it is possible to collect information about the pupils as to how much of vocabulary they have acquired during the six years of study of English as third language.

The survey method is broadly applicable to problems in many fields. Its capacity for wide application and broad coverage gives the survey technique its great usefulness in the behavioural sciences. The information that exists as it is, is studied through survey method. Kaushik (1974) employed this method for an investigation into the Basic Hindi Vocabulary of children of seventh class, Shastri (1972) used the survey method and testing procedure to study "The teaching of English as a second language with special reference to Structural Approach at work." Several others like George and Visveswaran (1967), Chadda (1971), Tejovathi (1988), etc. have used the survey method and testing procedures in their investigations related to English vocabulary.

Surveys depend on direct contact with those persons or a sample of those persons whose characteristics, behaviours or attitudes are relevant for a specific investigation. The survey method is used when the desired information can be obtained more easily and less expensively from other sources. In this method there is no need to have any controlled situation. The researcher is expected to go to the field to conduct a survey and that can be about anything. In view of the advantages of the survey method, the investigator selected the sample survey and testing procedures.

SELECTION OF THE SAMPLE

Sampling is an indispensable technique as the study of the large population is not possible. In this regard Fox (1969) says that "in all the social sciences, it is not possible to collect data from every respondent relevant to our study". There are various sampling procedures such as simple random sampling, systematic sampling, stratified random sampling, multiple or double repetitive sampling, multistage sampling etc. Subramanyam (1981) for his investigation made use of Stratified Random Samplings. For the present study the investigator made use of stratified random sampling technique as it was found to be more suitable for the study.

Stratified sampling is of three types namely disproportionate, proportionate and optimum allocation stratified sampling. The proportionate sampling refers to the selection from each sampling unit of a sample that is proportionate to the size of the unit. The school was taken as the unit in this study. Three districts in Andhra Pradesh, viz., Chittoor, Guntur and Krishna, were selected at random.

The data regarding the number of recognised high schools where the regional language is the medium of instruction in each of the districts was collected from the respective offices of the District Educational Officer (DEO). Stratification of the schools was made on the basis of the locality where they were situated. The schools situated in all the municipal towns and corporations were branded as urban schools and the remaining as rural schools. The distribution of schools under each strata in each district are shown in Table 4.5.

Table 4.5: Distribution of Schools in the Three Districts

Sl. No.	*Name of the District*	*Number of Schools*		*Total*
		Urban	*Rural*	
1.	Chittoor	30	261	291
2.	Guntur	64	252	316
3.	Krishna	81	200	281

The number of schools listed above is as per the information collected in the year 1985-86. From the total number of schools and the number of schools in each stratum a rough proportion was calculated. The distribution of schools selected for the study are presented in Table 4.6.

Table 4.6: Schools Selected for the Final Study

Sl. No.	*Name of the District*	*Number of Schools*		*Total*
		Urban	*Rural*	
1.	Chittoor	2	7	9
2.	Guntur	2	7	9
3.	Krishna	3	5	8

Size of the sample is an important aspect for the representativeness, a large sample is more likely to be a representative of the population. As the present study was done by the survey method a large sample was preferred. The total sample consisted of 1200 students of which there were 400 from each district and 40 to 50 from each school. The sample comprised both boys and girls.

Collection of Data

For the purpose of collecting data the investigator visited all the 26 schools in 3 districts personally. After having established sufficient rapport with the head of the institution the purpose of the visit was explained and requested for his/her cooperation in this regard. The heads of the institutions were kind enough to allow the investigator for collecting the necessary data from the students of X class. The investigator was introduced to the respective class teachers. With the help of the class teachers 40-50 students were selected at random from different sections of X class in the school.

The selected students were accommodated in a separate room comfortably. The purpose of the research was explained and interest was created among them in the task.

The vocabulary test consisting of 158 items was administered under the normal conditions of examinations. The students could complete the test roughly in about 2½ hours.

After the lunch break they were asked to assemble again in the same room. The self explanatory questionnaire in Telugu version was administered. Their doubts were cleared while they were answering different sections of the questionnaire. Care was taken to see that no student left any item unanswered.

On the following day about 20 students were selected at random from out of 40-50 students who served as the sample for the study for the purpose of administering the non-verbal mental ability test (RPM). Care was taken to include both boys and girls in the sub-sample of 20. The subjects were seated comfortably in the separate room and the booklets of RPM and answer sheets were distributed and they were given clear instructions to respond to the various items in the test.

Thus the required data for the study were collected from all the schools in about 3 months.

Scoring—Data

After completion of the data collection all the response sheets were carefully examined. The personal data and the responses of the subjects on all the tests were carried over to the tabulation sheets. The responses were converted into numerical scores with the help of the scoring key provided with each of the tests.

Coding of the Data for the Computer Analysis

The data was fed into the computer from the data sheets along with the standard statistical package programmes and results were obtained through the output. The various results obtained through computer analysis are discussed in the next chapter.

The high achievers in English vocabulary were identified on the basis of mean and standard deviation of the total sample, as found in the previous literature. The high achievers were those who scored above the value of mean + standard deviation and the low achievers were mean – standard deviation.

Statistical Methods Employed in the Analysis of the Data

The hypothesis of the investigation was proved as correct or incorrect by using suitable statistical techniques. The vocabulary test was valued with the help of the scoring key. The scores of the test were tabulated. Frequency distribution tables were prepared for the scores on vocabulary acquisition for the whole group and for the sub-groups like location-wise (urban/rural), sex-wise (boys/girls) and location combined with sex (rural boys, urban boys, rural girls, urban girls).

1. Measures of central tendency and dispersion were computed to examine the normality of the distribution.

2. Statistical graphs were drawn. The differences of means in the groups were tested for their significance or otherwise. Correlation matrices were computed to establish relationship between English vocabulary and non-verbal mental ability among the sub-groups for the sub-sample. Test of significance was used to accept or reject the hypothesis.

3. Chi square distribution and contingency tables were prepared to establish the relationship between vocabulary acquisition and other independent variables namely socio economic status, educational level of parents, general health, attitude, classroom instruction, home environment, leisure time activities, and psychological factors. The strength of the relationship was estimated by calculating the contingency coefficient for all the χ^2 tables.

4. Simple regression was used to find the nature of relationship between vocabulary and the other independent variables. The data were given for computer analysis.

5. Multiple Regression

Computer analysis was made use of to find the weightage of each factor in the development of English vocabulary.

Statistical formulae used in the course of analysis:

Means, standard deviation, mode, etc., were computed using the following formulae given in Garrett.

1. Mean = $AM + \Sigma \frac{fd}{N} \times i$

where Σ fd is the sum of the frequency multiplied by deviation, N is the number of cases and 'i' is the class interval.

2. Median = $l + \frac{\frac{(N\text{-}F)}{(2)}}{(fm)} \times i$

1 is the lower limit of the median class, N is the number of cases, *f*m is the frequency of the median class and F is the cumulative frequency and i is the class interval.

3. Mode = 3 Median − 2 Mean

4. Standard Deviation = $= \sigma = i\sqrt{\frac{\Sigma fd^2}{N} - C^2}$

where $\sum fds^2$ is the sum of the fd multiplied by d-deviations, N is the number of cases and C is = $\frac{\sum fd}{N}$ and 'i' is the class interval.

5. Skewness = $3\frac{(\text{Mean} - \text{Median})}{\text{S.D.}}$

6. Kurtosis Ku = $\frac{Q}{(P90 - P10)}$

7. Product Moment Coefficient of correlation for two variables:

$$r = \frac{\frac{\Sigma x'y'}{N} - C_x C_y}{\sigma' x \sigma' y}$$

The obtained correlation coefficients were tested for their significance referring to the correlation coefficients significance table in Garrett (1985, p. 201).

8. **Calculation of Critical Ratios:** To find whether there were significant differences between the mean performances of boys and girls, urban and rural residences in respect of the scores on vocabulary test and RPM test, the two tailed critical ratios were calculated. The formula used for calculation of critical ratio is as follows:

$$\sigma_D = \sigma(M1 - M2) = \sqrt{\sigma^2 M1 + \sigma^2 M2}$$

$$\sigma_D = \sqrt{\frac{\sigma^2 1}{N_1} + \frac{\sigma^2 2}{N2}}$$

(standard error of the difference between uncorrelated means)

in which

σ_{M1} = the SE of the mean of the first sample

σ_{M2} = the SE of the mean of the second sample

σ_D = the SE of the difference between the two sample means N_1 and N_2 = sizes of the two samples

CR = D/σ_D

The significance of the obtained CR was tested at 0.05 level and 0.01 level of probability. Among the table of 't' values for df = n-1 the critical ratios were found to be 1. 96 and 2. 58 at 0. 05 and 0. 01 levels respectively (Garrett 1985, p. 216).

9. Chi square distribution

χ^2 test of significance was used to investigate the relationship between the various independent variables on the one hand and the vocabulary on the other hand. To apply the χ^2 test the frequencies were arranged in (K × r) contingency tables where K is the number of columns and r is the number of rows.

$$\chi^2 = \Sigma\left(\frac{(f_o - f_e)^2}{f_e}\right)$$

where f_o = frequency of occurrence of observed or experimentally determined facts

f_e = expected frequency of occurrence on some hypothesis.

10. Contingency coefficients were also calculated to estimate the strength of relation between the two variables using the formula

$$C = \sqrt{\frac{\chi^2}{\chi^2 + n}}$$

where χ^2 = the chi square statistic obtained from the table and n is the total number of cases.

Chi square and critical ratios were computed with a calculator.

11. Percentages were calculated for a sub-sample of 200 cases for each item in the vocabulary test for the top 100 and bottom 100.

5

Analysis and Interpretation

This chapter deals with the analysis of the data using statistical techniques and the interpretation of the results.

The aim of the investigation was to study the nature of relationship between the acquisition of English vocabulary and other related factors and also to see if there was any significant difference in the acquisition of English vocabulary between boys and girls from rural and urban locality.

This chapter is divided into three sections. The first part is devoted to interpret the significant differences between the means of vocabulary scores among the sub-groups of sex and locale variables, The second part is concerned with discussion of the significant differences between means of the different levels of social and psychological factors in relation to the vocabulary scores. Correlation aspects are studied in the third section.

SECTION I

DESCRIPTION OF VOCABULARY ACQUISITION—VOCABULARY SCORES IN ENGLISH

The measures of mean, median, standard deviation, skewness, kurtosis and quartile deviations were found for the total sample comprising 1200 X class students. Table 5.1 shows the frequency distribution for it. The total average percentage scored by a student was 44.22. The range of vocabulary. scores was from 150 to 22. The highest score

Table 5.1: Distribution of Vocabulary Scores for the Total Sample

Class Interval	Mid Point	Freq. f	Cum. Freq.	Devtn d	Devtns fd	Devtns fd^2	Percentiles	Cum. % Freq.
150-159	154.5	1	1200	10	10	100	P 100=159.5	100.00
140-149	144.5	6	1199	9	54	486		99.88
130-139	134.5	18	1193	8	144	1152		99.38
120-129	124.5	27	1175	7	189	1323		97.88
110-119	114.5	28	1148	6	168	1008		95.63
100-109	104.5	72	1120	5	360	1800	P 90=103.94	93.30
90-99	94.5	101	1048	4	404	1616	P 80=90.78	87.30
80-89	84.5	132	947	3	396	1188	P 70=81.39	78.89
70-79	74.5	181	815	2	362	724	P 60=74.25	67.89
60-69	64.5	159	634	1	159	159	P 50=67.36	52.81
							P 40=59.81	
50-59	54.5	197	475	0	0	0	P 30=53.66	39.57
40-49	44.5	182	278	-1	-182	182	P 20=47.41	23.16
							P 10=40.82	
30-39	34.5	82	96	2	-164	328		8.00
20-29	24.5	14	14	-3	-42	126	P 0=19.5	1.17

(150) was secured by an urban girl and the lowest score (22) was secured by a rural boy. Over half of the vocabulary that was tested was known by 32.08% of the students. Nearly a quarter of the vocabulary was known by 76.83% of the students.

For the above frequency distribution of English vocabulary scores mean, median, mode, standard deviation skewness, kurtosis and quartile deviations were computed and presented in Table 5.2.

Table 5.2: Measures of Central Tendency and Measures of Variability

Sl. No.	*Measure*	*Value*
1.	Mean	69.98
2.	Median	67.36
3.	Mode	62.12
4.	Standard Deviation	24.69
5.	Skewness	6.31
6.	Kurtosis	.279
7.	Quartile Ql	50.61
8.	Quartile Q3	85.93
9.	Quartile Deviation	17.66

The measures of central tendency values disclose that the distribution is divergent from normal curve. The value of skewness supports the above inference. However the measures of dispersion reveal that 2/3 σ is almost equal to QD and the value of Kurtosis also indicates that the distribution is not abnormal. Hence it could be concluded that the distribution of scores follows normality with significant divergencies.

Between the mean and $\pm$ 1 σ lie the middle two-thirds (68.26% exactly) of the cases in the normal distribution. In the present investigation there are 828 cases between mean and $\pm$ 1 σ and this equals to 69%.

Between the mean and ± 2 σ are found 95 per cent (approximately) of the distribution. In the present study there are 1148 cases between mean and ± 2 σ and this is 95.67 per cent. Between the mean and ± 3 σ are found 99.7 per cent or very close to 100 per cent of the distribution. For this distribution it was found that there are 1197 cases between mean and ± 3 σ and its percentage is 99.75.

Graphs were drawn for the presented distribution of the total sample, Histogram, frequency polygon and cumulative frequency curves were drawn as shown in figure 1, 2 and 3 respectively. The distribution is found to be slightly positively skewed.

Sex and Vocabulary Acquisition

Among the entire sample boys and girls consisted 743 and 457 subjects respectively. The vocabulary scores of both boys and girls were formed into frequency distributions which are presented in table 5.4. The percentage cumulative

Figure 1
Histogram: Distribution of Vocabulary

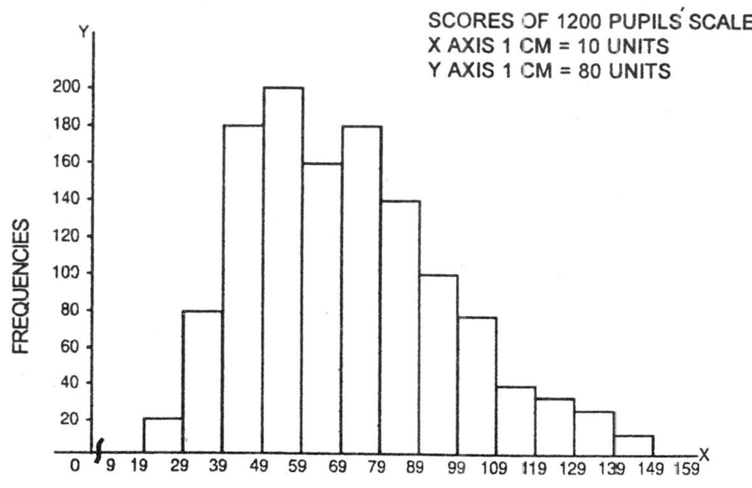

Figure 2
Frequency Polygon
(Data from Table 7)

* FOR DISTRIBUTION OF 1200 VOCABULARY SCORES

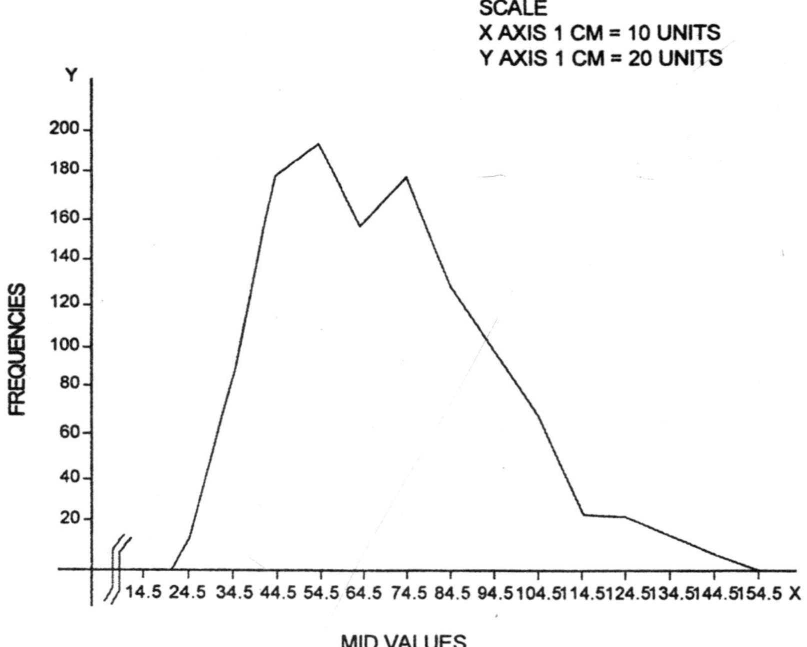

VOCABULARY SCORES

Figure 3
Cumulative Frequency Curve
(Data from Table 7)

FOR DISTRIBUTION OF 1200 VOCABULARY SCORES

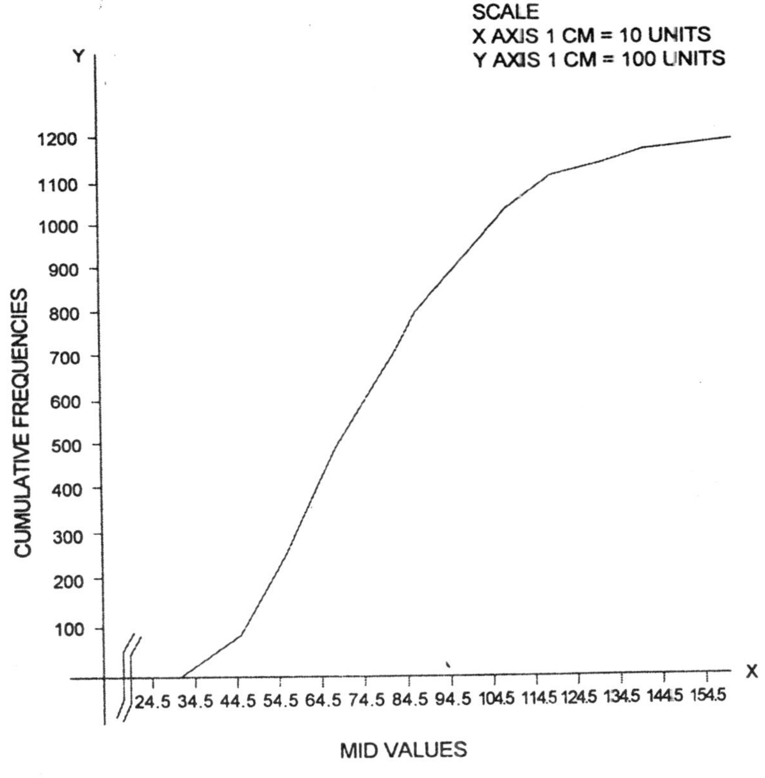

Table 5.3: Distribution of English Vocabulary Scores of Boys and Girls

Class Intrl	*Mid Point*	*Freq. Boys*	*Cum. Freq.*	*Cum. % Freq.*	*Freq. Girls*	*Cum. Freq.*	*Cum % Rreq.*
20 - 29	24.5	6	6	.81	8	8	1.25
30 - 39	34.5	52	58	7.81	30	38	8.32
40 - 49	44.5	121	179	24.09	61	99	21.66
50 - 59	54.5	115	294	39.57	82	181	39.61
60 - 69	64.5	97	391	52.62	62	243	53.17
70 - 79	74.5	100	491	66.08	81	324	70.89
80 - 89	84.5	86	577	77.66	46	370	80.96
90 - 99	94.5	73	650	87.48	28	398	87.09
100 - 109	104.5	44	694	93.41	28	426	93.22
110 - 119	114.5	17	711	95.69	11	437	95.62
120 - 12	124.5	18	729	98.12	9	446	97.59
130 - 139	134.5	12	741	99.73	6	452	98.91
140 - 149	144.5	2	743	-	4	456	99.78
150 - 159	154.5	-	-	-	1	457	-

frequencies were computed for both sex. These percentage cumulative frequencies are presented in Fig. 4. The ogives of the two distributions indicate that boys achieved almost at the same level as girls in their English vocabulary test.

Ogives were drawn for the two distributions of boys and girls. The two ogives merge into each other at the two extreme scores. The only place where they are a little apart is at the third quartile as is seen clearly in the Fig. 4.

Hypothesis—I

There would be no significant difference between boys and girls in the English vocabulary acquisition.

Means and standard deviations for boys and girls were computed. These values are presented in Table 5.4. The mean vocabulary score of boys is 70.19 and that of girls is 69.64. The standard deviation of boys is 24.65 and it is 24.74 for girls. However it is inferred that means of boys and girls do not deviate much from each other.

Table 5.4: Number Mean and Standard Deviations of Boys and Girls

No.	*Variable*	*Number*	*Mean*	*S.D.*	*Difference*	*"t"*
1.	Boys	743	70.19	24.65	0.55	0.39 @
2.	Girls	457	69.64	24.74		

@ = Not significant

* = Significant at 0.05 level

** = Significant at 0.01 level

The same notations are followed throughout the report.

The difference in the mean vocabulary scores of boys and girls was tested by using "t" test. From the table it was found that "t" value was not significant even at 0.05 level. Hence the null hypothesis that there would be no significant difference between boys and girls over their **English**

Figure 4
Ogives

COMPARISON OF SCORES MADE BY BOYS AND GIRLS

ON ENGLISH VOCABULARY TEST

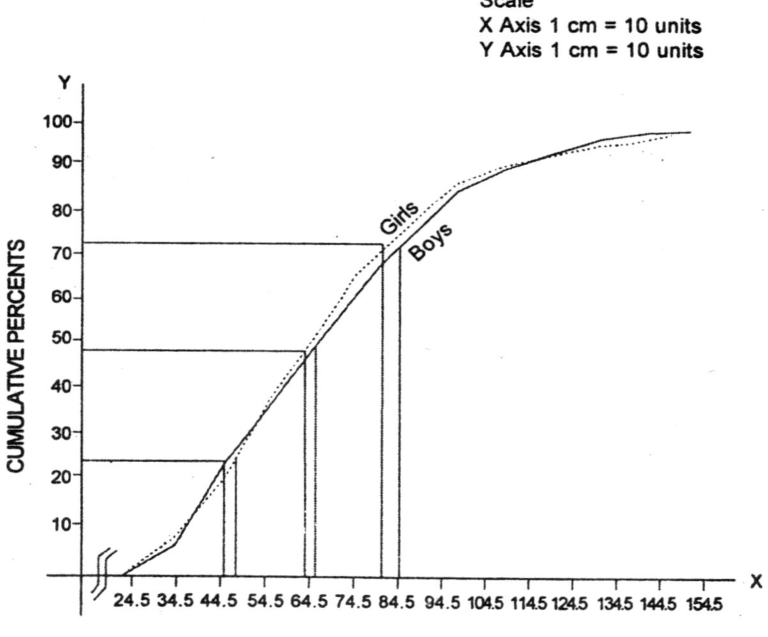

MID VALUES

Vocabulary Scores

vocabulary acquisition was accepted. There was no gender difference on the acquisition of English vocabulary. Girls were as bright as the boys in grasping and using English vocabulary.

Locality—English Vocabulary Acquisition

One of the prominent situational variables examined in the study is locality viz., urban and rural. Out of the total sample of 1200 children, urban subjects comprised 395 and rural children constituted 805. The vocabulary scores of both urban and rural sample were formed into frequency distributions which were presented in Table 5.5. The percentage frequencies were computed for both the groups and they were represented by ogives in Figure 5. Figure reveals that urban subjects showed better performance on vocabulary test than their rural counterparts.

Fig. 5 (graph) is an illustration which shows the ogives of the scores earned by the urban and rural children on the vocabulary test. Data from which these ogives were constructed is given in Table 5.5. The ogives of the urban children lies to the right of the rural over the entire range showing that the urban scored consistently higher than the rural. Differences in the vocabulary scores as between the two groups are shown by the distances separating the two curves at various levels. The differences at the extremes between the very high scoring and the very low scoring urban and rural are not so great as are differences over the middle range. The two groups differ more at the third quartile.

Hypothesis—II

There is no significant difference between urban and rural children in the acquisition of English vocabulary.

Means and standard deviations for urban and rural children were computed. These values are presented in Table 5.6. The mean vocabulary score of urban children was

Table 5.5: Distribution of Vocabulary Scores — Urban/ Rural Children

Class Intrl	*Mid Point*	*Freq. Urban*	*Cum. Freq.*	*Cum% Freq.*	*Freq. Rural*	*Cum. Freq.*	*Cum % Freq.*
20- 29	24.5	6	6	1.52	8	8	0.99
30- 39	34.5	23	29	7.34	59	67	8.32
40- 49	44.5	51	80	20.25	131	198	24.50
50- 59	54.5	64	144	36.46	133	331	41.12
60- 69	64.5	52	196	49.62	107	438	54.41
70- 79	74.5	53	249	63.04	128	566	70.31
80- 89	84.5	40	289	73.16	92	658	85.09
90- 99	94.5	28	317	80.25	73	731	90.81
100-109	104.5	28	345	87.34	44	775	96.27
110-119	114.5	17	362	91.64	11	786	97.64
120-129	124.5	18	380	96.20	9	795	98.76
130-139	134.5	10	390	98.73	8	803	99.75
140-149	144.5	4	394	99.74	2	805	-
150-159	154.5	1	395	-	-	-	-

Figure 5
Ogives

COMPARISON OF SCORES MADE BY URBAN AND RURAL STUDENTS ON ENGLISH VOCABULARY TEST

SCALE
X AXIS 1 CM = 10 UNITS
Y AXIS 1 CM = 10 UNITS

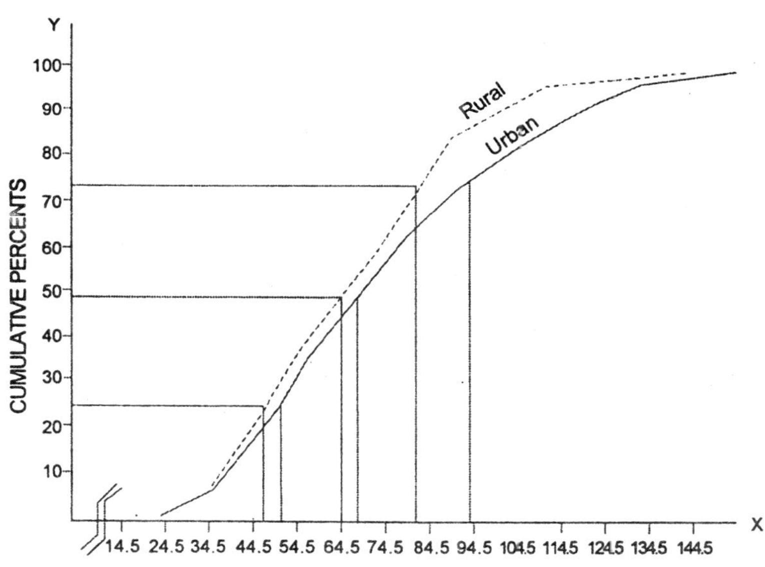

MID VALUES

VOCABULARY SCORES

73.97 and that of rural children was 68.03. The standard deviation of urban children was 27.7 and it was 22.82 for rural. Therefore it was inferred that mean scores of urban and rural children do deviate much from each other.

Table 5.6: Number, Mean and S.D. of Urban and Rural Children

No.	*Variable*	*Number*	*Mean*	*S.D.*	*Difference*	*"t"*
1.	Urban	395	73.97	27.70	5.94	3.69**
2.	Rural	805	68.03	22.82		

The difference in the mean vocabulary scores of urban and rural children was tested by using 't' test. From the table it was found that 't' value was significant at 0.01 level. Therefore the null hypothesis that there would be no significant difference between urban and rural children in their English vocabulary score was rejected.

It may be that the urban students have better opportunity to learn English vocabulary. The reason for this high achievement may be that they have educated parents, televisions, films and more scope to get into contact with English speaking society.

Hypothesis—II (a)

There would be no significant difference between urban boys and rural boys in the acquisition of English vocabulary.

Table 5.7: Number, Mean and S.D. of Urban and Rural Boys

No.	*Variable*	*Number*	*Mean*	*S.D.*	*Difference*	*"t"*
1.	Urban boys	213	76.37	27.98	8.67	4.02 **
2.	Rural boys	530	67.70	22.71		

Table 5.7 shows that the vocabulary mean score of the urban boys is higher than the mean score of the rural boys. There is significant difference between the two mean scores, the difference being 8.67 and the 't' value is found to be

4.02. It may be that the urban boys have more exposure to English vocabulary in the form of English newspapers, and other reading material available through public libraries, educated parents and neighbours etc., which the rural boys lack. Some of the rural boys might be burdened with house work like attending to cattle or helping father in agricultural work, after school time. Hence they may not have time to concentrate on learning English vocabulary. Therefore the rural school teacher must think of making arrangements for extensive reading within the school hours.

Hypothesis—II (b)

There would be no significant difference between the urban girls and rural girls in the acquisition of English vocabulary.

Table 5.8: Number, Mean and S.D. of Urban and Rural Girls

No.	*Variable*	*Number*	*Mean*	*S.D.*	*Difference*	*"t"*
1.	Urban girls	182	71.14	27.07	2.49	1.02@
2.	Rural girls	275	68.65	23.01		

Table 5.8 shows that there is no significant difference between the urban girls and rural girls in the acquisition of English vocabulary. There is a difference of 2.49 between the two mean scores and the CR value is 1.02 which is not significant even at 0.05 level. Hence the Hypothesis II (b) is accepted. The analysis of the scripts revealed that the urban girls had scored the highest marks of 150 and 148, and the rural girls scored 140.

It may be that the rural girls are hard working and hence there is no significant difference between the two mean scores.

Hypothesis—II (c)

There would be no significant difference between the urban boys and urban girls in their acquisition of English vocabulary.

Table 5.9: Comparison of Urban Boys and Urban Girls

No.	Variable	Number	Mean	S.D.	Difference	"t"
1.	Urban boys	213	76.37	27.98	5.23	1.884
2.	Urban girls	.182	71.14	27.07·		

Table 5.9 shows that there is no significant difference between the two mean scores at 0.05 level. Hence the hypothesis is accepted. The boys are superior to girls but this is not significant at 0.05 level. The mean score of the urban boys is the highest. It may be that in spite of the hard work that the girls usually do, the boys scored more. Perhaps the urban boys have more scope for wide exposure. The boys freely go to public libraries; they move freely in the English speaking society and they do not have any inhibitions. These factors may be responsible for their high scores. The highest score of 150 was scored by a girl. Whereas the girls because of the socio-cultural background do not go to the public libraries, they are shy and withdrawn and do not move freely with English speaking society.

Hypothesis—II (d)

There is no significant difference between the English vocabulary mean scores of rural girls and rural boys.

Table 5.10: Comparison of Rural Girls and Rural Boys

No.	Variable	Number	Mean	S.D.	Difference	"t"
1.	Rural girls	275	68.65	23.01	0.95	0.558@
2.	Rural boys	530	67.70	22.71		

Table 5.10 shows that there is no significant difference between the acquisition of English vocabulary of rural girls and rural boys. The difference between the two mean scores is negligible. Hence the hypothesis is accepted. The rural boys and the rural girls are at the same level in their learning capacity.

Bar Diagram Fig. 6, Mean scores in vocabulary for the mean scores of the variables in the vocabulary acquisition were represented in the Bar diagram. The figure shows that among them urban boys scored the highest with 76 as the mean and rural boys scored the lowest with 67 as mean.

COMPARISON THROUGH BAR GRAPHS
MEAN SCORES IN ENGLISH VOCABULARY-DIFFERENT SUBGROUPS

Figure 6

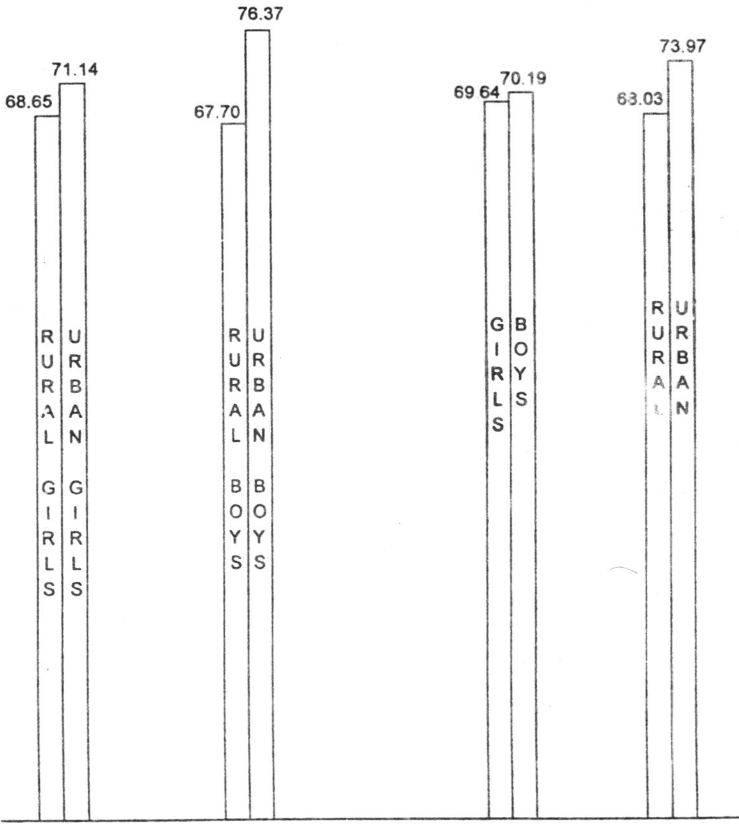

Details of performance on the vocabulary Test.

Hypothesis—III (a)

There would be no significant difference between the boys and girls, urban and rural students in the performance of the test items on identifying the meaning.

Table 5.11: Comparison of Means—Identification of Meaning

No.	*Variable*	*Number*	*Mean*	*S.D.*	*Difference*	*"t"*
1.	Boys	743	12.08	4.64	0.27	1.00@
2.	Girls	457	12.35	4.50		
3.	Urban	395	13.40	4.85	1.80	6.42*
4.	Rural	805	11.59	4.33		

Table 5.11 shows that there is no significant difference between the boys and girls in the performance on identifying meaning. Hence the hypothesis that there is no difference in the performance of boys and girls is accepted. The girls are as good as the boys in answering the questions on meaning identification.

There is significant difference in the mean of urban and rural children in the performance in identifying meaning. The urban students are superior to the rural students.

Hypothesis—III (b)

There would be no significant difference in the performance of the different variables in the question on identification of the problem from the clues given in context. All are same in their performance.

The Table 5.12 shows that there is significant difference between the performance of urban and rural students, urban boys and rural boys and rural girls and rural boys. The urban boys with a mean score of 16.67 scored the highest and the rural boys scored the lowest (13.55 mean score).

Table 5.12: Comparison of all Variables—Identifying One Word for Many

No.	Variable	Number	Mean	S.D.	Difference	C.R.
1.	Boys	743	14.44	6.11	0.40	1.11@
2.	Girls	457	14.84	6.06		
3.	Urban	395	15.97	6.88	2.05	5.17**
4.	Rural	805	13.92	5.49		
5.	Urban boys	213	16.67	7.14	3.12	5.77**
6.	Rural boys	530	13.55	5.39		
7.	Urban girls	182	15.16	6.47	0.54	0.915@
8.	Rural girls	275	14.62	5.77		
9.	Urban girls	182	15.16	6.47	1.51	2.22*
10.	Urban boys	213	16.67	7.14		
11.	Rural girls	275	14.62	5.77	1.07	2.609**
12.	Rural boys	530	13.55	5.39		

But there is no significant difference between the urban girls and rural girls, and the total boys and girls. There is significant difference between vocabulary mean scores of rural boys and rural girls at 0.01 level. But in the case of the mean score difference between urban and urban girls, it is significant at 0.05 level and not at 0.01 level.

Hypothesis—III (c)

There would be no significant mean difference in the performance of the different categories of students in the item on completion. All are the same in doing that part of the test.

From the Table 5.13 it is clear that the mean score in vocabulary acquisition is not the same for all the students. Hence the hypothesis III (c) is rejected. When it is concerned with rural urban differences, urban boys and rural boys, urban boys and urban girls, the mean difference is significant at 0.01 level. About the total sample of boys and girls, urban girls and rural girls, rural boys and rural girls, there is no significant difference. The mean score of the urban boys is the highest (19.39) and that of the rural girls is lowest (16.45).

Table 5.13: Performance in Completion

No.	*Variable*	*Number*	*Mean*	*S.D.*	*Difference*	*C.R.*
1.	Boys	743	17.368	7.208		1.562@
2.	Girls	457	16.735	6.58		
3.	Urban	395	18.367	8.29		3.93 **
4.	Rural	805	16.519	6.147		
5.	Urban boys	213	19.399	8.87		4.28 **
6.	Rural boys	530	16.55	6.23		
7.	Urban girls	182	17.159	7.376		1.085 @
8.	Rural girls	275	16.45	5.93		
9.	Urban boys	213	19.399	8.87	2.24	2.74 **
10.	Urban girls	182	17.159	7.376		
11.	Rural boys	530	16.58	6.23	0.1	0.223 @
12.	Rural girls	275	16.45	5.93		

Performances in different types of question items was done only for those sections which had more than twenty test items.

Percentages of correct responses to the vocabulary test were computed for five sections. They were calculated for each quartile and they are given in Table 5.14.

From Table 5.14 it is known that 50 per cent of the sample responded correctly to test items on meaning identification, one word for many and completion. The test items on word associations seems to be the best answered at the third quartile, but for the same one 0.42 per cent failed to produce even one correct response. In the definitions also 1.83 per cent of the respondents did not get one correct.

Table 5.14: Correct Responses to Five Sections of Vocabulary Test

Sl.	*Measure*	*Meaning Identifn %*	*One Word %*	*Completion %*	*Definition %*	*Association %*
1.	Quartile I	10.42	27.83	15.83	25.83	17.67
2.	Median	51.58	55.00	55.92	39.92	31.25
3.	Quartile III	31.17	15.75	24.25	23.83	34.25
4.	Above Q3	6.83	1.42	4.58	8.58	16.42
5.	No Score	-	-	-	1.83	.42

For the questions with less than ten items the percentages were worked out for each item separately as shown in the Table 5.15.

Table 5.15: Percentage of Correct Response for V to XI Questions

Ques. No.	*V Opposite %*	*VI Prefix Opp. %*	*VIII Suffix %*	*IX Suffix %*	*X Meaning %*	*XI Matching %*
1.	17.42	21.83	13.58	20.92	35	17.92
2.	19.92	29.42	16.67	24.83	-	26.08
3.	16.42	32.65	19.42	31.92	-	-
4.	16.92	-	19.17	-	-	-
5.	13.42	-	25.42	-	-	-
6.	7.75	-	-	-	-	-
No Score	8.17	16.08	5.75	22.33	65	56.00

From Table 5.15 it is clear that identification of meaning from the context was answered incorrectly by the highest per cent of the sample 65 and next comes matching with 56 securing no score. This shows that the item in section X of the question paper was difficult for the pupils. Among the opposites—the prefixes were answered incorrectly by most—it is 16.08 compared to the opposite words with 8.17 per cent incorrect. The prefixes and suffixes were also difficult. The teacher should give more practice on these items.

Itemwise Analysis of High and Low Achievers

From the total sample consisting of 1200 students belonging to urban and rural localities were separated. Among the two groups the boys and girls were identified. On the basis of the scores obtained by these four sub-groups the scripts of 25 high scorers and 25 low scorers were separated. Thus the top 100 and the bottom 100 achievers were considered for their performance on each item in the vocabulary test. The results are shown in Table 5.16.

Table 5.16: Performance of High and Low Achievers on Each Item

Item No.	*PL*	*PH*	*Item No.*	*PL*	*PH*
1.	36	67	17.	32	81
2.	56	94	18.	23	84
3.	46	80	19.	33	85
4.	38	87	20.	31	62
5.	25	73	21.	38	65
6.	41	96	22.	19	53
7.	32	71	23.	29	70
8.	38	80	24.	13	56
9.	38	82	25.	34	69
10.	36	67	26.	47	79
11.	14	59	27.	39	88
12.	25	56	28.	16	95
13.	35	53	29.	28	91
14.	29	88	30.	29	82
15.	32	96	31.	28	70
16.	33	88	32.	24	92

(Contd...)

Item No.	*PL*	*PH*	*Item No.*	*PL*	*PH*
33.	20	81	67.	18	54
34.	10	37	68.	24	58
35.	15	69	69.	24	87
36.	21	48	70.	38	95
37.	28	72	71.	45	97
38.	17	51	72.	32	90
39.	20	73	73.	8	65
40.	24	72	74.	38	87
41.	31	31	75.	25	75
42.	14	40	76.	18	63
43.	19	46	77.	20	85
44.	31	96	78.	25	51
45.	26	53	79.	19	78
46.	27	92	80.	28	53
47.	27	67	81.	26	34
48.	13	75	82.	20	52
49.	27	75	83.	30	47
50.	30	85	84.	20	72
51.	17	89	85.	25	81
52.	38	84	86.	17	63
53.	35	70	87.	22	60
54.	28	90	88.	17	67
55.	13	63	89.	22	68
56.	24	49	90.	23	76
57.	25	63	91.	15	85
58.	22	50	92.	13	67
59.	26	74	93.	18	32
60.	15	36	94.	22	25
61.	26	45	95.	26	94
62.	15	74	96.	24	75
63.	12	34	97.	25	85
64.	16	72	98.	35	75
65.	40	91	99.	29	40
66.	24	85	100.	40	82

(Contd...)

Item No.	PL	PH	Item No.	PL	PH
101.	17	73	130.	45	97
102.	19	90	131.	29	90
103.	36	46	132.	25	72
104.	21	32	133.	30	78
105.	20	33	134.	37	96
106.	20	83	135.	18	91
107.	29	89	136.	33	94
108.	18	56	137.	32	97
109.	20	75	138.	29	79
110.	39	97	139.	19.	97
111.	25	95	140.	28	98
112.	33	72	141.	35	97
113.	19	74	142.	26	91
114.	23	59	143.	36	92
115.	19	61	144.	23	78
116.	28	74	145.	34	90
117.	22	70	146.	38	100
118.	26	72	147.	39	98
119.	19	72	148.	38	97
120.	21	69	149.	29	95
121.	28	84	150.	36	98
122.	33	90	151.	23	85
123.	21	90	152.	24	90
124.	26	65	153.	36	95
125.	31	92	154.	24	81
126.	19	80	155.	33	81
127.	26	92	156.	28	60
128.	25	80	157.	19	63
129.	23	94	158.	14	69

On the whole, an item answered correctly by the high group was found to be answered correctly by at least 50 per cent from the low. There were some cases of equal performance of an item by the low and high groups. The word novel (item no. 146) was answered correctly by all the high achievers. Item No. 41 the word Encyclopaedia was performed correctly by the equal number of subjects from both the high and low achievers (31). The reason may be that one mostly refers to a dictionary and never to an encyclopaedia. Another pair of words tug (3) and constant (8) showed very little difference. It may be because the two words are from the passive vocabulary (item nos 94 and 81) the pupils might have encountered the words only in that passage and hence they failed to recall the meaning of the two words. Next pair of words with a difference of 11 (item nos 99 and 104) were the words "instruct" and "shower". These two words were answered correctly by PH 40 and PL 29 and PH 32 and PL 21 respectively. Perhaps their teacher used those words rarely. The words stray (item no. 93) and hesitate (item no. 105) are another pair of such words which differ by 14 and 13 respectively. We are familiar with the usage of a street dog more than a "stray" dog. The words "living" (item no. 63), "interrupt" (item no. 60), showed a difference of 21 and 22 respectively. For the words "dawn" and "gravity" the difference was found to be 27 and 26 (item no 34 and 42). Apart from that "dawn" was answered correctly by only 10 per cent from the low achievers.

The words in the low group which scored below 20 were studied. There were 24 such words. The difference between the high achievers and low achievers for these words ranged from 21 to 79 as shown in Table 5.17.

The words found in Table 5.17 seem to be very ordinary words. The high achievers had performed well but the low achievers failed to get the meanings of these words. A majority of the parents of low achievers had minimum education or no education at all and were of low socio-economic status. The parents education and their socio-economic status cannot be altered, but the teacher can pay special attention to such children and help learn English words better, through her/his novel techniques. The teacher can make them realize the value of learning English and doing self study for self improvement. The teaching material should be exploited fully first for it is a valuable guide both for the teacher and the student. It contains a number of

Table 5.17: Performance on Items by the Low Achievers Below 20

No.	Item Nos.	Diff between High and Low Achievers	Words
1.	91, 102, 28 139	70 - 79	Introduce, Lend, Widow Traffic.
2.	126	61	Success.
3.	62, 64, 73 79, 88, 92 101, 113, 119	50 - 59	Audience, Accident, Politics, Surrounded Citizenship, Shelter, Human being, Protect, Assistant.
4.	11, 24, 76 86, 115, 157	40 - 49	Dissolve, Link, Feats, Relative, Discuss, Matching Words - Radiator, Throat, Hollow, Horn.
5.	22, 67, 108	30 - 39	Delighted, Charge, Constitution.
6.	60	21	Interrupt.

activities, listening comprehension, speaking, teachers demonstration, role play and learning words. If the teacher were to practice these it would help the learner of any type (low SES or from uneducated family background).

The investigator collected information from the teachers through opinionnaire and personal interviews. The general feeling of the teachers was that the students are responsible for the low standards. In reality the students may not be having any interest, may not like the subject English because they fail to get the required marks for a pass. The teacher can create interest in the subject and also make the children have a positive attitude towards the English language.

The teacher has to be clear about his/her aims of teaching the new words. The quantity of new words is given in the course material itself. Some methods of teaching the new words are also suggested. If the teacher feels that the students could cope with a large vocabulary input, the teacher may decide to supplement the student's vocabulary from sources other than the prescribed course material. The students need frequent exposure and repetition of the new vocabulary. They must be given the opportunity to use the vocabulary as often as is necessary for recalling it at will.

Most of our students are not exposed to the English language outside the English class because of their low SES and low education of parents. Such children and even the others can be exposed to the English language in the form of appropriate reading material which is not too difficult and does not have too many difficult words. Wallace (1987) in his book Teaching Vocabulary comments that "students should be given access to books which are within their vocabulary range". This means a class library will be of much use to the children than the school library, it should have a range of reading materials, some easy enough for the weakest of them and others advanced for the better students. There are "haves" and "have nots" in the society as well as the class. The "haves" can be approached for contribution of books or money to furnish the class library. It can be worked out by the teachers. Thus with the self-furnished class library, the teacher can start a reading programme.

The students can read the books silently in the class and they can be encouraged to continue reading them at home. The teacher can keep a record of each student's reading—the number of books read and the titles. The students can be trained to do this work by filling a card with information about the book they read with a few comments on the book. This activity can be practised in any school in any place (urban or rural). If the students are initiated into this activity they will become masters of the language in no time.

The students can also be encouraged to maintain vocabulary cards. On the vocabulary cards they can write the word on one side and its meaning on the other side. The meaning can be in translation as well as the English language and also the usage of the word. They can arrange these cards alphabetically and use them as and when they need them. Sandosham (1980) points out that these vocabulary cards then become a kind of "word-bank" on which the learner draws according to his vocabulary needs.

Making posters related to a theme can be an interesting group activity. The posters would contain magazine cut outs with target language (English) equivalents. In the next stage the students can be encouraged to use these words in sentences both oral and written. For the vocabulary should as far as possible be learnt in contextual situation but not in isolation. There are many activities and exercises for the development of English vocabulary.

SECTION II

Analysis of the English Vocabulary and Mental Ability Scores

The Product Moment Correlation Coefficient was computed to find the relationship between the vocabulary acquisition and the mental ability. The mental ability test was administered to a sub-sample of 516 students from both rural and urban areas. The papers were valued. Those answer papers which were found to be inconsistent (according to the manual of RPM Test) were deleted from the calculation of correlation. The remaining papers were 478. For the sub-sample of 478, correlation coefficient "r" value was calculated by the product moment correlation. The scattergram was drawn. The correlation was calculated for other variables like boys, girls, rural and urban. The 'r' values are tabulated in Table 5.20.

Hypothesis—IV

There would be no significant relationship between the acquisition of English vocabulary and the non-verbal mental ability of the X class students.

Table 5.18: Correlation Value for the Subsample

No.	*Variable*	*number*	*r value*
1.	Sub-sample	478	.34 **

The significance of an obtained "r" may be tested against the hypothesis that the population "r" is in fact zero. To make the test the value of "r" is compared with the tabulated entries in Garrett (1985) p. 201. Two significance levels 0.05 and 0.01 are given in Table 25 of Garrett, which read as follows: r = 0.34 and N = 478. For 476 df the entries at 0.05 and 0.01 are by linear interpolation 0.0904 and 0.118 respectively. It is clear that the obtained r of 0.34 is much larger than 0.118, is highly significant at the 0.01 level. Therefore the null hypothesis that there will be no significant relationship between mental ability and acquisition of English vocabulary is not accepted. It means that there is positive close relationship between the mental ability and the acquisition of English vocabulary. If the students are superior in mental ability they are high achievers in English vocabulary.

The sub-sample of the mental ability group was further divided into three groups, high, average and low, based on the mean and standard deviation (SD) obtained in mental ability scores. The group with scores above mean + SD was designated as the high mental ability group and the group with scores below mean – SD was called the low mental ability group. The middle group was called the average mental ability group. For each group the vocabulary mean score and standard deviations were computed to test their significance or otherwise using 't' test. The values are given in Table 5.19.

From Table 5.19 it is clear that there is significant difference between the high mental ability group and the average and low. The high mental ability group is superior in the acquisition of English vocabulary also and it is significant beyond 0.01 level. This shows that the students

Table 5.19: Means, SD's, CR's of Scores of Performance in Vocabulary Test as Per Levels of Mental Ability

No.	*Level of Mental Ability*		*N*	*Mean*	*S. D.*	*Diff.*	*CR*
1.	a.	High	81	89.82	28.40		
	b.	Average	288	70.70	23.50	19.12	5.558**
2.	a.	High	81	89.82	28.40		
	b.	Low	109	66.14	21.47	23.68	6.28**
3.	a.	Average	288	70.70	23.50		
	b.	Low	109	66.14	21.47	4.56	1.839@

with high mental ability are definitely high achievers in English vocabulary too. Though there is an observed difference of 4.56 between the average and low mental ability group, it is not significant even at 0.05 level. Further "r" values were computed for the variables of sex and locale. They are tabulated in Table 5.20.

Table 5.20: Correlation Coefficient for Sex and Locale in Vocabulary and Mental Ability

No.	*Variable*	*Number*	*r value*
1.	Boys	271	.132
2.	Girls	207	.45 **
3.	Urban	201	.36 **
4.	Rural	277	.204 **

The values of "r" were compared to the table values in Garrett (1985, p. 201). The value for 269 df after interpolation was 0.1210 and 0.158 at 0.05 level and 0.01 level respectively. The value of "r" for boys was significant at 0.05 level only. The "r" values for girls, urban and rural children was significant beyond 0.01 level as they are above the values obtained by interpolation. This confirmed the earlier conclusion drawn that there was a significant positive correlation between non-verbal mental ability and English vocabulary acquisition. This was further analysed to find the mean difference of the vocabulary scores according to the levels of mental ability and the values are tabulated in Table 5.21.

Table 5.21: Mean, SD's, 't' Values for Vocabulary Scores of Different Levels of Mental Ability for the Sex Variable

No.	*Variable*		*Level of Mental Ability*	*Number*	*Mean*	*SD*	*'t' Value*
1.	Boys	*(a)*	High	52	85.12	26.20	
		(b)	Average	163	67.46	23.15	5.48**
		(a)	Average	163	67.46	23.15	
		(b)	Low	56	69.43	22.34	0.57@
2.	Girls	*(a)*	High	33	91.81	28.69	
		(b)	Average	128	75.81	24.52	2.93**
		(a)	Average	128	75.81	24.52	
		(b)	Low	46	60.72	19.31	4.18**

The means, standard deviations for the vocabulary scores of the three levels of mental ability viz, high, average and low were computed for both boys and girls. The obtained 't' values were compared to the table values in Garrett (1985). It was found that the high achievers in vocabulary do differ significantly from the average mental ability group.

However there is no significant difference between mean scores of the average and low mental ability groups of the boys. But, for the girls there is a significant difference between the means of the average and low mental ability groups also.

The mean and standard deviations in vocabulary were computed for the urban and rural children classified according to their mental ability. They are found in Table 5.22.

Table 5.22: Mean, SD's, 't' Values for Vocabulary Scores of Different Levels of Mental Ability for the Urban and Rural

No.	*Variable*		*Level of Mental Ability*	*Number*	*Mean*	*SD*	*'t' Value*
1.	Urban	*(a)*	High	38	85.24	28.67	
		(b)	Average	123	72.17	25.81	4.44**
		(a)	Average	123	72.17	25.81	
		(b)	Low	40	75.50	21.70	0.80@
2.	Rural	*(a)*	High	52	80.12	24.22	
		(b)	Average	166	69.96	22.77	2.63**
		(a)	Average	166	69.96	22.77	
		(b)	Low	59	72.11	19.25	0.70@

From Table 5.22 it was seen that mean vocabulary of the low mental ability group was a little higher than that of the average group but it was not a significant difference. The notion that high mental ability group were high achievers in vocabulary was found to be true as the 't' values show that they were significant beyond 0.01 level.

The analysis of the present study confirms the conclusions drawn in earlier studies about the relation between the mental ability and learning vocabulary.

Study of the Various Factors on English Vocabulary Acquisition—Chi Square

The Chi square test is an important test amongst the several tests of significance developed by statisticians. Chi square is symbolically written as χ^2. It is a statistical measure used in the context of sampling analysis for comparing a variance to a theoretical variance. As a non-parametric test it can be used to determine if categorical data shows dependency or the two classifications are independent. The test is a technique through the use of which it is possible for all researchers to (a) test the goodness of fit (b) test the significance of association between two attributes and test the homogeneity or the significance of population variance.

Chi square is an important non-parametric test and as such no rigid assumptions are necessary in respect of the type of population. As a non-parametric test χ^2 can be used (a) as a test of goodness of fit and (b) and as a test of independence.

As a test of goodness of fit χ^2 test enables us to see how well does the assumed theoretical distribution fit to the observed data. If the calculated value of χ^2 is less than the table value at a certain level of significance, the fit is considered to be a good one which means that the divergence between the observed and expected frequencies is attributable to fluctuations of sampling.

As a test of independence Chi square enables us to explain whether or not two attributes are associated. We frame the null hypothesis that two attributes are independent. On this basis, first the expected frequencies are calculated and then the χ^2 value is worked out. If the χ^2 value is less than the table value at a certain level of significance for a given degrees of freedom, it is concluded that the null hypothesis stands which means that the two attributes are not associated. But if the calculated value of χ^2 is greater than its table value our inference then would be that null hypothesis does not hold good which means the two attributes are associated, and the association exists in reality.

In the present investigation the Chi square test was employed as a test of independence to explain whether two attributes namely, vocabulary and education of parents, are associated or not. It was also used to confirm the conclusions drawn about vocabulary and the other independent variables like, socio-economic status, home environment etc. Two factors namely, general health and classroom activities, were left out as they showed low correlation values in the regression analysis. The tables with chi square values are given in the following pages.

The Educational Level of Family and Vocabulary Acquisition

Hypothesis—VI

There would be no relationship between the acquisition of English vocabulary and the educational level of the parents. The association between the two attributes was computed through Chi Square technique as shown in the Table 5.23.

Table 5.23: Chi Square—Education Level of Family and English Vocabulary

Description Level of Edn.	*Vocabulary Achivers*			
	High	*Average*	*Low*	*Total*
College education	89	197	24	310
High school	45	308	65	418
Elementary	62	323	87	472
Total	196	828	176	1200

$\chi^2 = 55.99^{**}$ C = 1.58

The Chi square value of 55.99 was obtained for the above table. It is found to be significant beyond 0.01 level. Hence the hypothesis that there would be no relationship between the educational level of parents and the acquisition of English vocabulary was rejected. Those parents who had college education were treated as the high group and children coming from the families of higher education seem to have more English vocabulary.

The mean, standard deviations in vocabulary were computed to see if there was any difference in the means of the children whose parents had college education and the others and the values were given in Table 5.24.

Table 5.24: Means, SD's, 't' for Different Levels of Education of Family

No.	*Level of Education*	*Number*	*Mean*	*S. D.*	*'t' value*
1.	*(a)* College	310	79.31	28.32	
	(b) High School	418	66.73	24.00	6.316 **
2.	*(a)* College	310	79.36	28.32	
	(b) Elementary School and Illiterate	472	66.87	23.02	6.45 **

As read from table 5.24 the number of parents who had college education was less compared to those who had high school and no education at all.

The mean of vocabulary score of the children whose parents had just high school education or even no education at all is almost the same, one being 66.73 and the other 66.67. The vocabulary mean of the children whose parents had college education was found to be 79.31. It may be that when parents have college education, they pay more attention towards the education of their children and at the same time insist that they learn English well. They may be helpful to their children by way of encouraging or explaining some difficult English words. They may be using English words now and then in their day-to-day conversation which the children also pick up unconsciously.

Attitude and Vocabulary Acquisition

Chi square value was computed for attitude and English vocabulary acquisition and it is tabulated in Table 5.25.

The obtained Chi square value of 24.46 indicates that there is association between the two attributes—vocabulary and attitude. A favourable attitude towards the learning of English vocabulary is associated with the acquisition of English words.

Table 5.25: Chi Square for Attitude and English Vocabulary

Description Attitude	*Vocabulary Achievers*			
	High	*Average*	*Low*	*Total*
Favourable Attitude	114	349	100	563
Unfavourable Attitude	82	479	76	637
Total	196	828	176	1200

$\chi^2 = 24.46^{**}$ C = .14

The Chi square was further analysed to compute the means and standard deviations for two groups of attitudes and the values are given in Table 5.26.

Table 5.26: Means, SD's, 't' Values of Vocabulary of the Students with Favourable and Unfavourable Attitudes

No.	*Attitude*	*Number*	*Mean*	*S.D.*	*'t' value*
1.	Favourable	565	71.46	27.14	2.216*
2.	Unfavourable	637	68.18	23.73	

The mean score of the group with favourable attitude was 71.46 and that of unfavourable attitude group 68.18. The difference between the two means was found to be significant at 0.05 level. Hence it may be concluded that a favourable attitude induces more learning to take place. This was also found to be true by George and Visweswaran (1967).

Home Environment and Vocabulary Acquisition

Chi square for the two attributes—vocabulary and home environment was found to be 15.18 which was significant at 0.01 level as shown in the Table 5.27.

Table 5.27: Chi Square for Vocabulary and Home Environment

Description Home	*Vocabulary Achievers*			
	High	*Average*	*Low*	*Total*
Very Conducive	42	114	30	186
Conducive	71	274	72	417
Not Very Conducive	83	440	74	597
Total	196	828	176	1200

$\chi^2 = 15.18$** C = .11

The Chi square value confirms the earlier conclusion arrived by the regression analysis that there was an association between English vocabulary and home environment. Children are motivated to learn more because of the encouragement and the better facilities that they get from their parents. Even if the parents do not have time to spare, a word of encouragement paves the way for greater learning to take place. Thus a more conducive home has its place in the acquisition of English vocabulary. The same was accepted by Pillai (1973) Jordon (1978).

This view is supported by Caroll (1967). The mean scores of the vocabulary for all the three groups of children were calculated and were found to be 73.02, 71.04 and 69.43. The χ^2 table shows that the highest number of students came from not very conducive home environment and it was nearly 50 per cent of the total sample.

Leisure Time Activities and Vocabulary Acquisition

Chi square for Leisure Time Activities and the acquisition of English vocabulary.

The Chi square value of 27.38 indicates that there is a good association between the acquisition of English vocabulary and leisure time activities. The list of leisure time activities that were given to the children were—reading

Table 5.28: Chi Square for Leisure Time Activities and Vocabulary

Description of Leisure Activities	*Vocabulary Achievers*			
	High	*Average*	*Low*	*Total*
Promoting Activities	33	91	38	162
Neutral	68	237	62	367
No Activities	95	500	76	671
Total	196	828	176	1200

$\chi^2 = 27.38$ * * C = 0.15

English books, preparing word lists while reading English books, reading small story books, cartoons, watching television, listening to English programmes, advertisements, listening to English radio lessons, watching English movies, doing crossword puzzles, participating in English drama etc. The number of students who use their leisure time in doing these activities was very low, it was 162 which was just 13.5 per cent and more than half 671 (55.9%) do not participate in any of the above mentioned leisure time activities. This shows that not many students get the scope to spend time and money to read English stories or magazines, or do crossword puzzles etc.

Chadda (1971) also says that "Reading habits of students and their attitudes towards English affect vocabulary. Students who read books, magazines and newspapers fared better on the test".

Psychological Factors and Vocabulary Acquisition

Chi square for Psychological factors and English vocabulary acquisition was computed and the results are tabulated in Table 5.29.

The Chi square value of 38.32 indicates that there is good association between the acquisition of English vocabulary and the psychological factors. Rauf (1976) in his

Table 5.29: Chi Square for Vocabulary and Psychological Traits

Description of Psychological Traits	*Vocabulary Achievers*			
	High	*Average*	*Low*	*Total*
Desirable	122	376	55	553
Neutral	64	363	94	521
Undesirable	10	89	27	126
Total	196	828	176	1200

χ^2 = 38.32 ** C =.175

book *Educational Psychology* observes that difficulties, inadequacies, insecurities, inferiority and frustration resulting from real or imaginary physical defects or deformities, previous experiences of school failure, humiliating attitudes of the teachers and classmates, interfere with the smooth learning among children. These are all psychological factors that affect learning. Hence in the learning of English words also these psychological factors interfere and they decrease the learning. The statements tested in this aspect were—on fear of English, despair, anxiety, fear of being laughed at to speak in English, learning English words causes anxiety etc. According to the investigation when the child had desirable psychological traits, the acquisition of English vocabulary was also found to be high.

The means and standard deviations were computed for the three groups in the psychological traits and they are given in Table 5.30.

As read from Table 5.30 the mean of the group with desirable psychological traits is higher than the other two groups and the difference was found to be significant. An understanding teacher can help the children in overcoming these psychological impediments, to facilitate the acquisition of more English vocabulary.

Table 5.30: Means. SD's, 't' Values in Vocabulary for Three Groups of Psychological Traits

No.	*Psychological Traits*	*Number*	*Mean*	*S.D.*	*'t' value*
1.	*(a)* Desirable Traits	553	76.85	24.96	
	(b) Neutral Traits	521	64.34	21.99	8.72**
2.	*(a)* Desirable Traits	553	76.85	24.96	
	(b) Undesirable Traits	126	62.51	22.64	6.29**

SES and Vocabulary Acquisition

Chi square table for socio-economic status (SES) and vocabulary are given in Table 5.31.

Table 5.31. Chi Square for SES and Vocabulary

Description of SES	*Vocabulary Achievers*			
	High	*Average*	*Low*	*Total*
High & Middle SES	138	433	73	644
Low SES	58	395	103	556
Total	196	828	176	1200

$\chi^2 = 33.23$ ** C = 0.19

The Chi square was first computed for three groups, the high socio-economic status group, the middle SES and low SES group. But only 3 frequencies were found in low vocabulary and high SES group, hence the high SES and the middle SES were combined together, as suggested in Garrett. The χ^2 value of 33.23 indicated that there was association between the socio-economic status and the acquisition, and it was found to be significant at 0.01 level. The same findings were revealed in simple regression analysis. The higher the socio-economic status the greater was the acquisition of English vocabulary. It may be that the children from high SES families have an advantage of greater scope for exposure to the English language. Lassman,

Fisch et al. (1980) found that individual differences in vocabulary are related to socio-economic variables such as parental income and occupation. The same truth is confirmed in this investigation also.

On the basis of the means and SD's "t" computed for the different SES groups, it can be stated that high SES groups are the high achievers in English vocabulary as given in Table 5.32.

Table 5.32: Means, SD's, Values for Vocabulary in the Different Levels of SES

No.	*Level of SES Traits*	*Number*	*Mean*	*S.D.*	*'t' value*
1.	*(a)* High SES	81	85.61	27.71	
	(b) Middle SES	563	22.90	24.84	3.907**
2.	*(a)* High SES	81	85.61	27.71	
	(b) Low SES	556	62.54	21.94	7.05**
3.	*(a)* Middle SES	563	72.90	24.84	
	(b) Low SES	556	62.84	21.94	7.18**

Table 5.32 shows that there is difference in the means of vocabulary of the high SES, middle SES and low SES. The high SES group has the highest vocabulary mean of 85.61. The difference is significant. The high vocabulary achievement may be due to better facilities available to children belonging to high SES group.

SECTION III

Simple Regression

Simple Regression Analysis was used to find the relationship between the dependent variable—English vocabulary and the other independent variables. In simple regression, there are only two variables at a time. One variable was the independent one which was the cause of the behaviour of another dependent variable. Regression can only interpret what exists physically i.e., there must be a physical way in which independent variable X can affect dependent variable Y. The basic relationship between X and Y is given by

$\hat{Y}=a+bX$

where the symbol $\hat{Y}$ denotes the estimated value of Y for a given value of X. This equation is known as the regression equation of Y on X, which means that each unit change in X produces a change of b in yl which is positive or direct and negative for inverse relationships. The regression analysis is a statistical method to deal with the formulation of mathematical model depicting relationship amongst variables which can be used for the purpose of prediction of the values of dependent variable, given the values of the independent variable.

Table 5.33: Simple Regression, Values for Vocabulary and Independent Variables, N = 1200

No.	*Variable*	*Correlation Coefficient r*	*T Values Transformed Values*	*Slope*
1.	Attitude	0.1056**	3.6761	0.5139
2.	Psychological factors	0.7956**	45.457	1.3615
3.	Socio-Economic Status (SES)	0.7896**	44.53	0.0291
4.	Home Environment	0.0538*	1.8643	0.0917
5.	Leisure Time Activities	0.0494@	1.7115	0.1129
6.	General Health	0.035@	1.2129	0.3242
7.	Classroom Activities	0.0013@	0.0456	0.0032

In the present investigation the investigator used the simple regression to express the relationship between the dependent variable and the other independent variables namely, socio-economic status, general health, classroom activities, home environment, leisure time activities and psychological factors. Prediction was not attempted in this study. The data was fed into the computer and the results tabulated in Table 5.33.

The "r" value for 1000 is read as 0.062 and 0.081 at 0.05 and 0.01 levels respectively from Garret page 201. The value of "r" by interpolation for 1198 df is 0.051 and 0.0676 at 0.05 and 0.01 levels respectively.

Hypothesis—V

There would be no significant relationship between the acquisition of English vocabulary and the socio-economic status (SES) of the X class students.

As is evident from Table 5.33 the socio-economic status (SES) of the parents has a high degree of correlation with the acquisition of English vocabulary. The obtained value for SES was 0.7896 which is far above the interpolated value of 0.0676 at 0.01 level. Hence the hypothesis that there would be no relationship between SES and English vocabulary is rejected. The higher the socio-economic status the more will be the acquisition of English vocabulary. Dawson (1963) has pointed out that SES has a strong influence on vocabulary. It may be that the parents of high socio-economic status can provide better learning facilities in the form of more exposure to the English language through audio-visual aids like television or radio or tape recorder, story books in English or newspapers etc. It may be that parents make use of English words at home in their conversations with their children. They have the finance to engage a tutor or arrange for tuition in school, while children from low SES cannot afford to.

Hypothesis—VII

There would be no significant relationship between the acquisition of English vocabulary and the general health of the pupils of X class.

The correlation coefficient value obtained for this significant variable was 0.035. This value was below the required value of 0.51 at 0.05 level. So it showed that there was correlation but it was very low and hence statistically it was not significant at 0.05 level. Hence the hypothesis that there would be no relationship between English vocabulary acquisition and the general health of the children was accepted. All the 1200 students were more or less in good health. They did not have any impediments of vision or hearing or speech.

As per the information collected from the English teachers in rural schools, in general the rural students were poor in English because of their irregular attendance, which was not only due to ill health but also because of the agricultural seasonal work which drew the children away from school.

The teachers expressed their inability and helplessness in controlling the continuous absence from school. They said that even the parents were not willing to send the children to school during the time of harvest of various crops because it was an additional source of income which they could not afford to lose. Their real interest seemed to be in earning rather than learning, as earning was their immediate need. The reason behind this was poverty. With the cost of living rising day by day the search for other sources of income is also a part of daily life for survival.

Hypothesis—VIII

There would be no significant relationship between the acquisition of English vocabulary and the attitude of the X class students.

The obtained value of correlation coefficient for the dependent variable and the independent variable—attitude, is 0.1056. Compared with the interpolated value for 1198 df which is 0.051 and 0.0676 at 0.05 and 0.01 levels, the "r" value obtained is high above the two levels. Hence there is a high degree of association between attitude and the acquisition of English vocabulary. The hypothesis that there would be no significant relationship between the two variables vocabulary and attitude is rejected. The obtained "r" value indicates that they are significant beyond 0.01 level. Positive attitude towards the teaching and learning of English words may increase the learning capacity. Thus a positive attitude towards English and interest in the subject are helpful in building up the pupils vocabulary. Spolsky (1969) in his study on "Attitudinal Aspects of Second Language Learning" pointed out that attitude does increase the learning ability.

Hypothesis—IX

There would be no relationship between the acquisition of English vocabulary and the classroom teaching activities of the X class students.

The correlation coefficient value was 0.0013. It was a positive value but very low and it was not significant even at 0.05 level. Therefore the hypothesis that there would be no relationship between the acquisition of English vocabulary and the classroom activities is accepted. In the next stage the investigator went through the responses of the students about the teaching of English vocabulary and the techniques and audio-visual aids used by the teacher. Students of the same section taught by one teacher had responded in different ways to the statements. There was no agreement about the audio-visual aids used by their teacher among the students. The perceptions about the teaching of the teacher differed from student to student.

Spolsky (1969) in his study on Attitudinal aspects of Second Language says that "among the factors that have been proposed as significant are method, age, aptitude and attitude. Of these teaching method has generally been considered the most easily controllable but results of research into the effectiveness of various methodologies have generally proved to be disappointing". The major two year study by Scherer and Wertheimer (1964) showed that there was no real difference between audio-lingual method and traditional approach to teaching German in college. It may be that the classroom teaching studied by using the statements given to the students was not effective. The reason also may be that the individual differences in the learners may have lead them to respond in different ways, for a fast learner one or two aids or even no use of audio-visual aids might have meant much to him, and served as a learning model. The same may not be true about a slow learner. He may need something more to be motivated to learn.

Hypothesis—X

There would be no relationship between the acquisition of English vocabulary and the home environment of the X class students. The table value of "r" as obtained by regression is 0.0538. This value is found to be significant at 0.05 level. It is clear that there is some association between home environment and the acquisition of English vocabulary. Hence the hypothesis that there would be no relationship between the home and the acquisition of English vocabulary is rejected. Better home environment, a conducive home or good climate in the home may effect the pupils English vocabulary. When parents encourage and support the children, then more learning takes place. Better home climate increases the learning and retaining of more English words. Shah (1984) on Study of the Effect of Family Climate on students said "the role of parental encouragement in the area of academic success was found to be important". The same truth is established in the present Study. This was emphasised by Jordon (1978).

Home is the place where children spend most of their time. If parents take interest in their children's education, sit with them to help them in learning new English words or to understand what they already learnt in school, the children will benefit a lot. They may at least encourage their children to listen to English programmes broadcast over the radio, television etc. Caroll (1967) in his study on foreign language found that "one reason why some students reach high levels of attainment in a foreign language is that they have home environments that are favourable to this, either because the students are better motivated to learn or because they have better opportunities to learn". A word of encouragement from the parents does a lot of good to the learner and is motivated to learn.

Hypothesis—XI

There would be no significant relationship between the acquisition of English vocabulary and their leisure time activities.

The leisure time activities are undertaken by the children in their own free time. The relation between the leisure time and vocabulary was found to be positive. The obtained value of 0.0494 is nearer to the value of 0.051 which is the required value of "r" at 0.05 level. Hence it may be inferred that there is some association between English vocabulary and leisure time activities but it is not significant at 0.05 level. Activities that promote the learning of English such as reading English story books and other English reading material, doing English crossword puzzles, listening to English programmes, singing or listening to English songs, etc., may influence the learning of English words. Khanna and Agnihotri (1982) say that "reading English books he will certainly have higher scores in English". Through such leisure time activities the students are exposed to more English. The more the input the more will be the learning. When the input is in different ways, the intake and hence learning of new words will be more. Music in language Teaching has its influence on vocabulary "the singing of songs ... are important to the study of language both in their vocabulary and content" says Chandy (1980).

Hypothesis—XII

There would be no relationship between the acquisition of English vocabulary and the psychological factors of X class students. The correlation coefficient 'r' value obtained for the two variables namely psychological factors and English vocabulary is 0.7956. This value is much above the value of 0.0676 required for significance at 0.01 level. Hence the hypothesis that there would be no relationship between English and psychological factors is rejected. There is a high degree of association between vocabulary acquisition and the psychological factors. As Krashen (1983) in his "Input hypothesis and the teaching of EFL" has put it, "the lower the level of anxiety the more will be the learning". Factors such as fear and shyness will reduce intake which in turn may affect the learning of new words in English. The constant fear that English is a difficult subject and that it cannot be learnt may reduce the learning capacity. Someone who is self conscious may be unwilling to try to produce unfamiliar sounds in another language and may not want to sound like a speaker of another language.

Multiple Regression

Multiple regression is defined as the correlation between scores actually earned on the criterion and scores predicted in the criterion from the multiple regression equation. The multiple regression equation is mainly used for two purposes — (1) analysis and (2) prediction. In the analysis, the purpose is to determine the importance of "weights" of each of a number of variables in contributing to some final result.

This analysis is adopted when the research has an independent variable which is presumed to be a function of two or more independent variables. The objective of this analysis is to make a prediction about the independent variable based on its co-variance with all the concerned independent variables. One can predict the level of the dependent phenomena through multiple regression analysis model—given the levels of independent variables. The regression coefficients viz. bl, b2 become less reliable as the degree of correlation between the independent variables (viz, X1, X2) increases. If there is a high degree of correlation between independent variables, there is a problem of what is commonly described as the problem of multicollinearity. It is said that by adding a second variable, say X2, that is correlated with the first variable, say X, distorts the values of the regression coefficients. Prediction can be made even when multicollinearity is present, but in such a situation, care should be taken in selecting the independent variables to estimate a dependent variable so as to ensure that multicollinearity is reduced to the minimum. When the regression equation contains 4 or 5 variables, additional tests lead to negligible increases in multiple (R).

Given a dependent variable, the linear multiple regression problem is to estimate constants B1, B2. . . . . BX and A such that the expression Y = Bl Xl + B2 X2 +. . . . score based on his X scores.

In practice, Y and the several X variables are converted to standard scores ZY1, ZY2. . . . Zk each Z has a mean of 0 and standard deviation of 1. Then the problem is to estimate constants B1 such that Z1 = B1 Z1 + B2 Z2 +. . . standardized Y score, Zy. The expression on the right side of the above equation is the linear combination of explanatory variables. The constant A is eliminated in the process of converting X's and Z's. The least squares method is used to estimate the beta weights in such a way that the sum of the squarred prediction errors is kept as small as possible, i.e., the expression E (Zy – Zyl)2 is minimized. The predictive adequacy of a set of beta weights is indicated by the size of the correlation coefficient rZyl Zly between the predicted Zyl scores and the actual Zy scores. This special correlation coefficient from Karl Pearson is termed the multiple correlation coefficient (R). The squarred multiple correlation, R2, represents the proportion of criterion (Zy) variance accounted for by the explanatory variables, i.e., the proportion of total variance that is "Common Variance".

In the present investigation the computerised technique was used to compute multiple regression. The vocabulary (test score) was taken as dependent variable and the other factors namely attitude, classroom, home environment, leisure time activities, psychological factors, socio-economic status etc., were taken as the independent variables. The computer output results are as follows:

The per cent of variation attributable to the regression (R2) was found to be 15.26. This indicated that there were some factors which were not included in this study which might be responsible for the development of English vocabulary. It may be that the value was low because there were many other variables acting on the dependent variable and they were not studied in this investigation. One of the factors—the education of parents—could not be included as the scores for that variable were tabulated separately as the number of columns were 25 and this could not be accommodated along the same horizontal line in the computer analysis. Another problem was that the mental ability scores were there for only 518 subjects. The value obtained for correlation computed through product moment method indicated that there was a positive high degree of correlation between the mental ability and vocabulary acquisition.

In the next step one independent variable namely mental ability was deleted and the per cent of variation attributes to the regression was found to be 13.62. Among the factors studied 1.64 per cent of variance was caused by the effect of mental ability.

With the socio-economic status as the Independent variable and the acquisition of English Vocabulary as the dependent variable, the per cent of variation attributable to the regression was found to be 5.56. This value increased to 12.15 with the inclusion of the independent variable named Psychological Factors. This shows that in the acquisition of English Vocabulary 6.59 per cent is attributable to Psychological factors. The inclusion of other factors namely leisure time activities, home environment, classroom activities, attitude and general health caused negligible increase in the per cent of variation attributable to the regression.

Therefore the English teachers should try to make the student to feel interested in the class. He/she should help the students to overcome these psychological impediments which are blocking the learning of English words.

Table 5.34: Correlation Matrix

	Voca	*Intel*	*GH*	*Atti*	*CR*	*HE*	*LTA*	*PF*	*SES*
Vocabulary	1								
Intelligence	.17	1							
General Health	.04	.02	1						
Attitude	.11	.04	.05	1					
Classroom	.00075	.05	–.03	.29	1				
Home Environment	.05	.04	–.04	.45	.28	1			
Leisure Activities	–.02	.016	–.01	.47	.32	.74	1		
Psychological	.28	.08	.04	.11	.03	.04	–.01	1	
SES	.24	.12	–.03	.15	.06	.35	.24	.12	1

From the correlation matrix it was found that the intercorrelation between home environment and leisure time activities was significantly high. This means that a rich home environment can provide good leisure time activities which together will increase the English vocabulary of the students. Hence parents must take interest in their children's learning activities and encourage them so that they may increase their vocabulary.

There was good correlation between home environment and attitudes. This shows that better home environment will develop in the children favourable attitude towards learning English words. When there is favourable attitude, this will increase the learning capacity of the learners.

Socio-economic status and home environment also show a fairly good association. Students from high socio-economic status have a very conducive home environment and the two factors together are likely to increase the English vocabulary of the pupils.

The other inter-correlations among the different social and psychological factors were found to be very feeble.

6

Summary, Conclusions and Recommendations

INTRODUCTION

"Language is a steed that carries one into a far country" says an Arab Proverb (Fromkin, et al., 1986: p. 260). The world is full of people speaking different languages. In many areas a single language is often used as a link language and in India English has been playing the role of a link language. A study conducted by Shaw (1979) on students from Hyderabad city in India, revealed that the students studied English because they used it for jobs and because it was there in the system of education. They also felt that the English language made them better persons. From the reasons given by the students it can be said that they were generally learning English for instrumental purposes. If the language is being used for such a purpose to fulfil an educational requirement, to get a better position and to read material in the language, then it is being learnt for instrumental purposes.

English is an international language. Nehru described it as the window of the world, if we close this window we would be in darkness. The advancements in Science and Technology are taking place at a very fast pace, the learning of English will enable us to catch up with the rest of the world.

The knowledge of English is an asset to the Indian student. Knowledge of a language demands mastery of its vocabulary. Sufficient vocabulary is necessary to master the sound system and the structures of any language. As English now has the role of a library language, what our students need is a mastery of the vocabulary. Knowing a language itself means knowing the words of that language. In learning a second or third language, we begin to attach fresh labels to familiar things and ideas. The more the input the better the vocabulary. The input of the English language may take place in the English classroom, at home, in the library and in better social environments. The process of development of the language can be facilitated or retarded according to how regularly input takes place.

Vocabulary is an important aspect of language. A person's knowledge depends on the bulk of English vocabulary he possesses. The success of an individual is governed by his vocabulary. It develops one's command over the language and this gives him confidence. Lack of stock of words or inability to recall the correct words, makes one inefficient in expression, be it oral or written.

For the Indian students good command in English vocabulary is an asset in their higher education and will be very useful in their professional life. In view of the need and importance of the acquisition of English vocabulary it is felt that the factors contributing to the improvement or development be studied.

Intelligence is a major contributing factor in the acquisition of English vocabulary. What the child gains from his environment is conditioned by his capacity to learn. McCarthy (1954) found that there is considerable evidence to indicate a marked relationship between socio-economic status of the family and the child's linguistic development. A healthy and conducive home environment does provide special opportunity to learn more English vocabulary. Jordon (1978) found that certain aspects such as parents encouragement of the child's verbalisation, conversation, word games, reading to the child and provision of reading materials would influence vocabulary attainment.

The physical and mental health do affect the development of vocabulary. Impaired vision or hearing decreases the vocabulary intake. When the student is absent from class for many days due to ill health, he does not get the clear understanding of the new vocabulary, that is presented in the class by the teacher because classroom is the only place to hear English for most of our students.

Another contributing factor in vocabulary growth is the attitude and interest a child has developed towards the subject. Upshur (1968) and Spolsky (1969) have proved that positive attitude to the second or foreign language leads to high attainment of that language. Spolsky's study reaffirmed the importance of attitude as one of the factors explaining degree of proficiency a student achieves in learning a second language.

Among the factors being studied, the classroom instruction that the child receives in the usage of new words and phrases is the most important.

Home is the place where the pupil has more opportunities to improve his knowledge. Whatever the parents say or do draws the attention of the child. The home conditions can facilitate the pupils learning of the English vocabulary. If the parents speak to the child in English or encourage the pupil to read English books or listen to Radio and Television programmes in English, this will naturally be another source of English vocabulary.

Outside the classroom the child has his own leisure time. The leisure time can be spent in reading English newspapers or comics or magazines or doing crossword puzzles etc. These activities are very interesting and at the same time the pupil will learn unconsciously. Leisure time activities contribute to the development of vocabulary. If the child learns under stress and fear complex, then learning becomes secondary. The fear of the subject and the emotional toils connected with it will draw the student away from the English class. This movement will gradually increase the distance between the teacher and the taught and it will become an obstacle in the process of learning.

The Problem and its Significance

Right perceptions are necessary among the teachers and parents about the various factors involved in the development of the pupils vocabulary. After the shift in the emphasis of English from the first language to third language position, there is a steady decline in the standard of English. Adequate command in the vocabulary will help to decrease this decline. Therefore there is need to find out the ways of developing the pupils' English vocabulary. The parents and teachers who are responsible for the future of the pupils can help them, only when they know the important factors that contribute to the development of the English vocabulary of the pupils. Hence the problem chosen for the study is "A Study of the Acquisition of Active and Passive Vocabulary in English of the Students of X class in Relation to Certain Social and Psychological Factors". The passive and active vocabulary are together referred to as vocabulary as there are only 36 words and they were not separately tested.

Here Vocabulary is inclusive of both active and passive vocabulary, all the 395 words in the text book are tested only at the recognition level and not at production level.

The X class was taken for the study as it is the last year of the schooling, and more learning takes place at this stage and before this stage.

Objectives of the Study

The focus of the study was mainly on the factors contributing to the acquisition of the pupils English vocabulary. The present study therefore aimed at the answers to the following questions:

1. What is the extent of vocabulary acquisition of X class pupils?

2. Is there any difference in the acquisition of English vocabulary between boys and girls?
3. Is there any difference between the English vocabulary acquisition of students in urban and rural areas?
4. What is the relationship between the following factors and the acquisition of English vocabulary?
   - *(a)* Socio-economic status of parents.
   - *(b)* Education of the parents.
   - *(c)* General health of the pupils.
   - *(d)* Pupils attitude to the English reader and subject and words.
   - *(e)* Classroom teaching activity.
   - *(f)* Home environment, i.e., encouragement.
   - *(g)* Leisure time activities.
   - *(h)* Psychological factors.
   - *(i)* Pupils mental ability.

Variables Studied

1. Dependent Variable: English Vocabulary.
2. Independent Variables:
   - *(a)* Socio-economic Status
   - *(b)* Education of Family
   - *(c)* General Health
   - *(d)* Attitude
   - *(e)* Classroom Activities
   - *(f)* Home Environment
   - *(g)* Leisure Time Activities
   - *(h)* Psychological Factors
   - *(i)* Mental Ability
   - *(j)* Sex
   - *(k)* Locality

Tools Used

1. ***Vocabulary Test*** - An objective type multiple choice test consisting of test items suggested by various language testing experts such as Lado (1970), Harris (1969), Valette (1977) etc. was constructed. The test items were of the following types:

   (i) *Identification of meaning* - The most suitable meaning to the problem word was to be identified,

   (ii) *One word for many* - One word that could replace the group of words in a sentence was to be identified,

   (iii) *Completion* - A word suitable to complete the sentence was to be found,

   (iv) *Definition* - A word to match the definition supplied was to be selected,

   (v) *Word association* - The word that could be associated with the problem word was to be found,

   (vi) *Antonyms* - The word that would mean the opposite of the problem word was to be identified,

   (vii and viii) *Prefixes and Suffixes* - for the incomplete word the correct prefix or suffix was to be supplied,

   (ix) *Context* - For the problem word from the different meanings, the meaning based on the context was to be identified,

   (x) *Matching* - the problem word was to be matched with its meaning, the correct response was to be selected from the matched patterns given.

In all 371 test items were constructed for 395 words out of which 158 items (164 words) were selected for the final test.

2. ***Questionnaire*** - The questionnaire was divided into different sections to collect information about the factors that contribute to the development of the English vocabulary. All the factors included under the independent variables were considered.

3. The Raven's Progressive Matrices were used to measure the mental ability.

Sample

A sample of 1200 respondents was selected on the basis of random stratified proportionate sampling procedure. Three districts namely Chittoor, Guntur and Krishna were selected at random. From each district 400 students were selected at random.

Administration of the Tools (Final Study)

Prior permission was taken from the Heads of Institutions and the class teachers for administering the test. The vocabulary test comprising 371 test items prepared on the basis of the 395 words in the IX class reader used during 1985-89 was given to 400 students. The test was conducted in four separate sittings. The answers were evaluated and the marks were entered. The scripts were arranged from the highest to the lowest marks. From the analysis of the top 100 and the bottom 100 scripts, item difficulty and discrimination values were calculated using the formulae given in Harper and Harper (1990, pp. 358, 360). The number of items selected with good discrimination and difficulty index came to 158. The questionnaire was also administered in the pilot study, necessary changes were made in the final form of the questionnaire.

The finalised vocabulary test and questionnaire were administered to 1200 pupils.

Scoring

The vocabulary test was scored with the help of the scoring key. The marks were tabulated. The different sections of the questionnaire were analysed separately. Points were given to decide the socio-economic status, education of the parents, and the general health of the pupils. For other sections in the questionnaire namely attitude, classroom teaching, home environment, leisure time activities and psychological factors—the five point scale was used. The mental ability test was scored with the help of the scoring key provided in the manual of the Raven's Progessive Matrices.

Statistical Procedures Used

The various statistical techniques used for the analysis of the data are:

1. Mean, median, mode, standard deviation, quartile deviations, and skewness for the vocabulary test.
2. "t" test to compare the vocabulary means of the variables.
3. Product moment correlation to find the relation between the mental ability and vocabulary scores.
4. Simple regression to establish the relation between the dependent variable and the independent variables—general health, attitude etc.
5. Chi square to find the association between the dependent and independent variables.
6. Multiple Regression to identify the contributing factors to vocabulary learning and to find which factor has more influence on the acquisition of English vocabulary.

Findings

1. The analysis of the data revealed that there is significant difference between the rural and urban students in the English vocabulary test. The urban

children were found to be superior to the rural children in the acquisition of English vocabulary. Even among the urban, the boys scored more than the girls. But the highest score of 150 was secured by a girl. The assumption that there is no significant difference between the rural and urban children in the acquisition of English vocabulary was not accepted.

2. The correlation matrix showed that there is a significant relationship between mental ability and the acquisition of English vocabulary. The hypothesis that there is no relationship between mental ability and the vocabulary acquisition was not accepted.

3. The Chi square test revealed that there is an association between the acquisition of the English vocabulary test and the socio-economic status (SES) of parents. It was found that SES does influence vocabulary acquisition. The high achievers in vocabulary test belonged to the high SES group and the middle SES group scored average marks in vocabulary. A majority of the low achievers were from the low SES group. The hypothesis that there is no relation between vocabulary and SES was not accepted.

4. From the Chi square test it is found that there is a high degree of association between the English vocabulary and the level of education of parents. Children whose parents had college education were found to be superior in vocabulary. The children whose parents had just high school or elementary education and no education secured less than the high group. Therefore the hypothesis that there is no relation between English vocabulary and the educdtion of parents was not accepted.

5. The relationship between attitude and English vocabulary was found by the Chi square test. The test revealed that there is association between English vocabulary and attitude. Children who had positive

attitude that is those who liked their English reader, class, learning English words, etc., scored more in vocabulary test. Hence the hypothesis that there is no relation between attitude and English vocabulary was not accepted.

6. The Chi square test for the acquisition of English vocabulary and home environment revealed that there is an association between the two. The children who received parental care, attention, help and encouragement were found to be superior in vocabulary. The children who were left to themselves had scored less. As such the hypothesis that there is no relation between English vocabulary and home environment was not accepted.

7. Leisure time activities and its relation to English vocabulary was found through Chi square test. The result showed that there is a good association between English vocabulary and leisure time activities. Children who participated in activities such as reading English books, comics, small story books, autobiographies, watching T.V. programme and listening to English programme over the radio, listening to English songs, doing English cross words, jumbles, riddles, writing letters to pen friends in English etc., were found to be superior in English vocabulary. Therefore the hypothesis that there is no relation between English vocabulary and leisure time activities was not accepted.

8. The relation between English vocabulary and psychological factors was studied by the Chi square test. The result revealed that there is association between the two factors. Children who did not have fear, despair, anxiety about the English class, who did not feel shy to converse in English, etc., had secured good marks in English vocabulary. Hence the hypothesis that there is no relation between English vocabulary and the psychological factors was not accepted.

9. Simple Regression analysis was done for the English vocabulary and the other independent variables namely SES, general health, attitude, classroom activities, home environment, leisure time activities and psychological factors. The results of the analysis revealed that there is a relationship between English vocabulary and SES, attitude, home environment, leisure time activities and psychological factors. There was very low correlation between English vocabulary and the general health of the pupils, and there was almost no relation between the vocabulary and the classroom activities. The points given to classroom activities were studied and it was found that the pupils from the same school, same class taught by one teacher, responded to the statements in different ways. There was no uniformity in their views about the classroom activities. Their perceptions about the teaching of English differed.

10. Multiple Regression was done to find the contribution of each factor to the acquisition of English vocabulary. In this study Psychological factors was found to have more weight. Inter and Intracorrelations were also obtained. The intercorrelation between home environment and leisure activities was high. There was good association between home and SES and home and attitude. The other intercorrelations were feeble.

Educational Implications

The overall analysis of the findings of the study led to certain inferences that can be applied to the classroom situation and the individual pupils and parents to improve the English vocabulary of the secondary school leavers (X Class).

The English teacher can try to remove the fear about the English language, and the feeling that English is a difficult subject. The pupils can be given the opportunity to make use of the words in the class, the students can be asked to frame sentences with the new words orally in the class.

The teacher in the rural schools must devote more time to teach new words and teach them in an interesting way. The first thing that the rural teacher says is — "our students are poor in English". The teacher attributes this to the rural environment and the limited exposure that the child gets. The teacher can make the class into a place of wide exposure, by using pictures and objects.

The teacher has to change his attitude and make the class more interesting by making use of the simple visual aids like—flash cards, word charts, sentence charts, tables with words and word families, objects available within the school campus like—books, pens, flowers, leaves, small stones, the classroom situation etc. The teaching of English words ought to be combined with real language context and the teacher should be innovative in this regard. Pupils could be made to develop increased interest in reading and proper self study habits. They should be given training in exploiting the informal sources of language learning like—books, magazines, story books, radio, television and co-curricular activities. They could be given practice in identifying words of different kinds—homophones, homonyms similarly affixed words etc.

The teacher could check the pupils progress now and then and encourage the pupils to do more. The learning of English vocabulary is also influenced by the attitude of the learner. If the learner is alert, attentive and interested in the material to be learnt, he is bound to have a favourable attitude towards it. Such an attitude will enable him to tackle the learning situation economically, pleasantly and effectively.

Desirable emotional conditions (in this study they are organised under psychological factors) enhance the speed of learning. This could be applied to the learning of English vocabulary. Happiness, joy and satisfaction are always favourable for any type of learning. Adverse emotional factors would hinder learning. Many studies have established the fact that emotional strain, stress, tensions, disturbances etc., are extremely crucial to scholastic pursuits. The most common emotional provocations are—inferiority complex, frustration, previous experiences of school failure, humiliating attitude of the teachers and classmates etc.

A considerate teacher can locate the pupils suffering from these emotional impediments to learning English and help them to overcome these obstacles.

The role of family expectancy forces encouragement for the acquisition of English vocabulary. Child's learning is greatly influenced by the ambitions, aspirations and encouragements of the parents.

The investigator observed that the class reader contains a number of exercises to reinforce the vocabulary that is introduced. But the students are not trained to work out these exercises independently. The teacher just dictated the answers or they found answers in the guides. From the oral information collected from the teachers while administering the test, it was known that the teachers do not make use of any audio-visual aids even though they are available. The investigator found the teacher making use of the radio lesson for Social Studies, the same teacher expressed inability to use radio lesson in English. Their reason for not using was that they found the radio lessons to be difficult to follow.

The analysis of the test revealed that in general the pupils were poor in the use of the antonyms, prefixes and suffixes. The teacher can take more care about these aspects of the English vocabulary. They can be taught through language games.

As Lake (1967) puts it "Every classroom teacher should be virtually interested in establishing a firm base upon which the child might learn to build his vocabulary". The natural process of acquiring a good vocabulary is by absorbing words steadily from extensive reading. Since children spend comparatively less time in reading, the teacher can assign herself on to this by incorporating more vocabulary through games and puzzles—for children respond easily to them.

LIMITATIONS AND SUGGESTIONS FOR FURTHER RESEARCH

1. This study was limited to Chittoor, Guntur and Krishna districts of Andhra Pradesh. Similar studies can be undertaken covering other districts in the state and it can be extended to other states.

2. The present study was limited to X class pupils. This could be extended to all the classes from VI to X. The sample was selected from only schools where the regional language was the medium of instruction. This could be extended to schools where English is the medium of instruction.

3. The present study was limited to the study of the words in IX class reader. This study could be extended by taking into consideration words from the readers of VI class to X class.

4. In the present study the active and passive vocabulary were treated together as one. This could be done in a systematic manner by conducting separate test items for the active and passive vocabulary, so that they could be studied in comparison.

5. The present study did not classify the acquisition of vocabulary according to the classification of words into structural words and content words. The study on vocabulary could be done for both structural and content words.

6. The present study about the independent variable was limited to statements about hearing, vision and general health, all taken together as one. This could be done in a systematic way by dividing this part into different sections—hearing, vision, etc., and each one could be treated as a separate variable.

7. The present study about the vocabulary acquisition did not consider the attainment in the parts of speech like nouns, verbs, prepositions etc. This could be done by giving test items separately on the parts of speech.

8. In the present study the distribution of vocabulary in each unit, in the Reader was not studied. A study could be done on the distribution of words in each unit and analysed for the grading and selection of vocabulary.

9. The study was limited to vocabulary acquisition as indicated by the ability of the pupil to understand the usage in context, antonyms and definitions, and not a mere test of comprehension. The test was constructed by including certain items where more than one alternative was found to be acceptable answer. The future researchers may construct such items with an instruction to the subjects to identify the most appropriate alternative instead of a correct one. This study could be undertaken by taking up the vocabulary acquisition at the production level. The study was confined to the vocabulary that was given in their text-book.

10. To measure the mental ability of the students RPM Raven's Progressive Matrices was used in the present investigation although this test measures only the visual relations, a part of mental ability. Future researchers may include other tests of intelligence (which cover different factors of intelligence) to identify its influence on vocabulary acquisition.

Bibliography

Agnihotri, R. (1979) "Language Development among Infants in Relation to their Social Strata". In *Third Survey of Research in Education*. Ed. M.B. Buch (1986) NCERT, New Delhi. p. 581.

Amoriel, J.W. and Donald B.H. (1984) "Vocabulary Development—Contextual and Morphemic Cueing". *Reading World*. May.

Ashworth, Mary (1985) *Beyond Methodology*. Cambridge University Press, Cambridge.

Atkinson, Pressley and Levin, K. Delaney (1986). *The Handbook of Research on Teaching*. Ed. Merlin C. Wittrock. Macmillan and Co., New York.

Balajathy, E. (1988). "An Investigation of Learner Control Variables in Vocabulary Learning using Traditional Instruction and two forms of Computer based Instruction". *Reading Research*, Quarterly. 27:4. pp. 15-24.

Ballard, P.B. (1964). *Teaching and Testing English*. University of London Press Pvt. Ltd., London.

Barnard, Helen (1961). "PUC Students' Vocabulary", *CIEFL Bulletin* 1: p. 90.

Bhal, J.D. (1975). "Study of the Vocabulary in Gujarathi of Pupils of Std. VI in Saurashtra", In *Second Survey of Research in Education*. Ed. M.B. Buch (1979). Society for Educational Research and Development, Baroda. p. 585.

Bhishikar, L. (1980). "An Experimental Analytical Study of the Acquisition of Reading Skills". In *Third Survey of Research in Education*. Ed. M.B. Buch (1986) NCERT, New Delhi. p. 583.

Birley, Rosalind (1988). *Improve Your Word Power*. Hugo's Language Books Ltd., London.

Bloomfield, Leonard (1933). *Language*. Holt Rinehart and Winton, New York.

Bower, G.H. and Karlin, M.B. (1974). "Depth of Processing Pictures of Faces and Recognition Memory". *Journal of Experimental Psychology,* 103, pp. 751-57.

Bradfield, Moreduck (1957). *Measurement and Evaluation in Education*. Macmillan & Co., New York.

Brooks, Nelson (1964). *Language and Language Learning: Theory and Practice*. Harcourt, Brace and World Inc., New York.

Bullard, N. (1985). "Word Based Perception - A Handicap in Second Language Acquisition". *ELT Journal*. 39:1. January. pp. 28-31.

Carrol, J.B. (1964) "Words Meanings and Concepts". *Harvard Educational Review*. 34.

Carrol, J.B. (1967). "Foreign Language Proficiency Levels Attained by College Majors near Graduation". *Foreign Language Annals,* 1 : 2, pp. 131-151.

Carrol, J.B., Peter Davies R Barry Richman (1971). *Word Frequency Book*. Houghton Miffin, Boston Mass.

Carter, Ronald (1987). "Vocabulary". *Applied Linguistics*. Allen and Unwin Pvt. Ltd, London.

Chadda, Usha. (1971). *An Investigation into Vocabulary Resources of Third Year Degree Students*. Unpublished Dissertation, P.G. Research Diploma, Central Institute of English and Foreign Languages, Hyderabad.

Chandrasekharaiah (1964). "An Investigation of the Basic Vocabulary in Kannada of Elementary School Children of Std. I to VII of Mysore State". In *Second Survey of Research in Education*. Ed. M.B. Buch. (1979). Society for Educational Research and Development, Baroda.

Chandy, V. (1978). "Control over Structure and Vocabulary". *Journal of Educational Research and Extension*. 14 : 3. January.

Chandy, V. (1980). "Songs in the English Classroom". *Journal of English Language and Teaching.* 15:1-6.

Chandy, V. (1980). "The Treatment of Vocabulary". *Journal of English Language and Teaching.* 15 : 1-6.

Clark, E.V. (1973). "The Children's Acquisition of Semantics in His First Language". *Cognitive Development and Acquisition of Language.* Academic Press, New York.

Coomber, E.J., Ramstad, D.A., Sheets, D.A.R. (1986). "Elaboration in Vocabulary Learning—A Comparison of three Rehearsal Methods". *Research in the Teaching of English".* 20 : 3. pp. 281-293.

Craik, F.I.M., and Lockhart, R.S. (1972). "Levels of Processing: a Framework for Memory Research." *Journal of Verbal Learning and Verbal Behaviour.* II. pp. 599-607.

Dahl, Hartwig (1979). *Word Frequencies of Spoken American English.* Verbatim, Essex, Conn.

David, Annie (1983) "A Viable Theory of Testing Vocabulary". *CIEFL Bulletin.* 19 : 2. pp. 61-67.

Davis, E.A. (1976). *Louisana the Pelican State.* Baton Rouge, L.A., Lousiana State University Press. Lousiana.

Dawson, A. Mildred and Marian Zollinger (1963). *Guiding Language Learning.* Harcourt Brace & World Inc., New York.

Day, R.R., Omura, C., and Hiramatsu, M. (1991). "Incidental EFL Vocabulary Learning and Reading". *Reading in a Foreign Language,* 7 : 2. pp. 541-547.

Dickinson, D.K. (1984). "Children's Knowledge of Words Gained from a Single Exposure—First Impression". *Applied Psycholinguistics.* 1 : 6. pp. 359-375.

De Cecco, John (1977). *The Psychology of Learning and Instruction.* Prentice Hall of India, New Delhi.

Deighton, L.C. (1960). "Developing Vocabulary: A look at the Problem". *English Journal.* 49. pp. 82-88.

Desai, M. M. "Learning Words". *Journal of English Language Teaching*. 15 : 2, p. 57.

Deutsch, M. (1965). "Minority Groups and Class Status as Related to Social and Personality Factors in Scholastic Achievement", *Society of Applied Anthropology*, Monograph, No. 2, Ithaca, New York.

Dippie, H. (1977). In "Teaching English Vocabulary". *Teaching of English in India*. Sachdev, M.S. (1977). Parkash Brothers, Jullundur.

Di Vesta, F.J. & Peverly, S.T. (1984). "The Effects of Encoding Variability, Processing Activity and Rule Examples Sequence on the Transfer of Conceptual Rules". *Journal of Educational Psychology*. 76. pp. 108-119.

Dwivedi, R.K. (1987). *Study of Words: A Generative Vocabulary*. A Monograph. Gurukul Publications, Lucknow.

Ebel, L. Robert. (1951). *Measuring Educational Achievement*. Prentice Hall of India, New Delhi.

Edgar, Dale. (1965 a). "Vocabulary Development of the Underprivileged Child". *Elementary English*, 42 : 11, pp. 778-785.

Edgar, Dale. (1965 b). "Vocabulary Measurement and Major Findings". *Elementary English*, 42 : 12.

Elley, W.B. (1989). "Vocabulary Acquisition from Listening to Stories". *Reading Research Quarterly*, 24, pp. 174-87.

Emig, J. (1977). "Writing as a Mode of learning". *College Composition and Communication*, 28, pp. 122-128.

Festinger, Leon. (1976). *Research Methods in the Behavioral Sciences*. Amerind Publishing Co. Pvt. Ltd., New Delhi.

Fielden, R.D.S. and Hill, L.A. (1962). *Vocabulary Tests and Exercises for Overseas Students*. Oxford University Press, London.

Filmore, N.G. (1956). *Vocabulary Exercises for First Year Juniors*. George G. Harret & Co., London.

Fowler, H.W. (1965). *Teaching Languages: Composition and Literature*. McGraw Hill, New York.

Fox, D.J. (1969). *The Research Process in Education*. Holt Rinehart and Winston, New York.

Fox, W.J. (1974). "Building Vocabulary". *English Language Teaching Forum*. July/September.

Fromkin, Victoria and Robert Rodman (1986). *An Introduction to Language*. CBS Publishing, Japan. p. 260.

Gaikwad, M.A. (1982). "A Comparative Study of Efficacy of the Direct Method and the Bilingual Method of Teaching English to Lower Classes of Secondary Schools in Rural Areas of Maharashtra". In *Third Survey of Research in Education*. Ed. M.B. Buch (1986) NCERT, New Delhi. p. 587.

Gardner, R.C. (1960). *"Motivational Variables in Second Language Acquisition"*. Dissertation. McGill University.

Gardner, R.C., Smythe, P.C. and Clement, R. (1979). "Intensive Second Language Study in a Bicultural Milieu: An Investigation of Attitudes, Motivation and Language Proficiency". *Language Learning,* 29 : 2, December.

Garrett, H.E. (1985). *Statistics in Psychology and Education*. Vakils, Feffer and Simons Ltd., Bombay.

Gatenby, E.V. (1970). "Reasons for Failure to Learn a Foreign Language". *ELT Selections-I*. Ed. W.R. Lee. Oxford University Press, London.

George, P.A. and Viswesaran, H.V. (1967). "An Investigation of the Acquisition in English upto the end of Standard V of Children Studying in VI Standard, 9+". *Journal of Educational Research and Extension,* 4 : 1, July. p. 31.

Giri, B.G.P. (1976). "Construction of Vocabulary Test in Hindi for the Purpose of Classes VI through X". Unpublished Dissertation, Patna University, In *Second Survey of Research in Education*. Ed. M.B. Buch. (1979) Society for Educational Research and Development, Baroda.

Gleason (1987). *Vocabulary*. Applied Linguistic Perspectives, by Ronald Carter. Allen & Unwin Publishers, London.

Goode and Hatt (1952). *Methods in Social Research*. McGraw Hill, New York.

Gravenall, Betty. (1970). "Music in Language Teaching". *ELT Selections-I.* Ed. W.R. Lee. Oxford University Press, Oxford.

Greene, H.A., Albert, N.J., Raymond, G. (1954). *Measurement and Evaluation in the Elementary School.* Longman's Green and Co., New York.

Halverson, R. (1985). "Culture and Vocabulary Acquisition". *Foreign Language Annals,* 18 : 4. p. 327.

Harmer, J. (1983). "Krashen's Input Hypothesis and the Teaching of EFL". *World Language English,* 3 : 1. pp. ll-15.

Harper, E.A. and Harper, E.S. (1990). *Preparing objective Examinations: a Handbook for Teachers, Students and Examiners.* Prentice Hall of India, New Delhi.

Harris, A. and Milton J. (1972). *Basic Elementary Reading Vocabularies.* Macmillan, New York.

Harris, P., David (1969). *Testing English as a Second Language.* McGraw Hill Book Co. Ltd., New York.

Harvey, P.D. (1983) "Vocabulary Learning—The use of Grids". *ELT Journal,* 37 : 3.

Heaton, J.B. (1975). *Writing English Language Tests.* Longman, London.

Hubbard, P., Hywel, J., Thornton, B. and Wheeler, R. (1986). *A Training Course for TEFL.* ELBS Oxford University Press, Oxford.

Hyde, T.S. and Jenkins, J.R. (1969). "Differential Effects of Incidental Tasks on the Organisation of Recall of a List of Highly Associated Words". *Journal of Experimental Psychology.* 82, pp. 472-481.

International Encyclopaedia of Education. (Ed.) Torsten Husen and Postlethwaite, N. (1985). Pergamon Press, Oxford.

Jenkins, J.R. and Pany, D., and Schreck, J. (1978). "Vocabulary and Reading Comprehension—Instructional Effects". *ERIC* Document Reproduction Service No. ED 160 999.

Jennifer, S. (1972). "Sociolinguistic Review of the Iowa Test of Basic Skills". *Language and Linguistics Working Papers.* No. 5. George Town University, Washington. pp. 61-64.

Jiganti, M.A. and Tindall, M.A. (1986). "An Interactive Approach to Teaching Vocabulary". *The Reading Teacher.* 39 : 5, January. pp. 444-448.

Jordon, T.E. (1978). "Influences on Vocabulary Attainment: A Five Year Prospective Study". *The International Encyclopaedia of Education.* Ed. Torsten Husen and T. Neville Postlethwaite. Pergamon Press, Oxfords. 9:T-Z, pp. 5468.

Joshi, T.L.S. (1986). "English Necessary for New Knowledge". *The Progress of Education,* LX : 8, p. 195.

Kaushik, J.N. (1974). "An Investigation into the Basic Hindi Vocabulary of Children of VII class in the State of Haryana". In *Second Survey of Research in Education.* Ed. M.B. Buch. (1979). Society for Educational Research and Development, Baroda.

Kelley, T.L. (1939). "The Selection of Upper and Lower Group for the Validation of the Test items". *Journal of Educational Psychology,* 30, pp. 17-24.

Kern, G.R. (1989) "Second Language Reading Strategy Instruction : Its Effects on Comprehension and Word Inference Ability". *Modern Language Journal,* 73 : 2 pp. 135-148.

Keskar, K.A. (1972). *A 3500 Word Vocabulary for the Teaching of English in Indian Schools.* Central Institute of English and Foreign Language, Hyderabad.

Khanna, A.L. and Agnihotri, R.K. (1982). "Language Achievement and some Social Psychological Variables". *CIEFL Bulletin,* 18 : 1 and 2, pp. 41-51.

Konopak, B.C. (1988). "Eighth Grader's Vocabulary Learning from Inconsiderate and Considerate Text". *Reading Research and Instruction,* 27 : 4, pp. 1-14.

Koppar, B. (1970). "An Enquiry into Factors Affecting Reading Comprehension (in English)". Ph.D. Edn. MSU, In *Third*

Survey of Research in Education. Ed. M.B. Buch (1986) NCERT, New Delhi. p. 592.

Kotakgira, H. (1981). "Development of a Course for Increasing the Reading Proficiency in English of the Post High School Students of Gujarat". In T*hird Survey of Research in Education*. Ed. M.B. Buch (1986) NCERT, New Delhi. p. 593.

Kothari, C.R. (1990). *Research Methodology*. Wiley Eastern India Ltd., New Delhi.

Krashen, S.D. (1979). A Response to McLaughin. "The Monitor Model: Some Methodological Considerations". *Language Learning*. 29 : 1, pp. 151-68.

Krashen, S.D. (1983). 'The Input Hypothesis' In J.W. Oller Jr. (ed.): *Issues in Language Teaching Research,* Newbury House, Rowley, Mass.

Kumar, V.R. (1982). "Assessment of Entering Behaviour in English of Pupils of Std. VIII". In *Third Survey of Research in Education*. Ed. M.B. Buch (1986) NCERT, New Delhi. p. 603.

Lado, Robert (1964). *Language Teaching: A Scientific Approach*. McGraw Hill Inc., New York.

Lado, Robert (1970) *Language Testing*. Longman, London. p. 1, 22-25, 321.

Lake, M.L. (1967). "First Aid for Vocabularies". *Elementary English,* 44 November. p. 783.

Lambert, W.E. and Gardner, R.C. (1959). "Motivational Variables in Second Language Learning". *Canadian Journal of Psychology*. 13.

Lassman, F.M. Fisch et al. (1980) "Early Correlates of Speech and Language Hearing": *The Collaborative Perinatal Project of National Institute of Neurological and Communicative Disorders*. PSG Publishing, Little Town, Massachusetts.

Levin, J.R. and Carney, R.N. (1988). "Facilitating Vocabulary Inferring through Rootword Instruction". *Contemporary Educational Psychology,* 13. pp. 316-322.

Lindeman, H.R. (1971). *Educational Measurement*. B. Taraporevala Sons & Co., Bombay.

Lindstromberg, S. (1985). "Schemata for Ordering the Teaching and Learning of Vocabulary". *English Language Teaching Journal*. 39 : 4, October.

Martin, M. (1984). "Advanced Vocabulary Teaching : The Problem of Synonyms". *The Modern Language Journal*, 68 : 2.

Marzano, J.R. (1984). "A Cluster Approach to Vocabulary Instruction: A New Direction from the Research Literature". *The Reading Teacher*. November.

McCarthy (1954). In *The Foundation of Language: Talking and Reading in Young Children"*. By Andrew Wilkinson (1984), Oxford University Press, Oxford. p. 95.

Mezenski, Karen (1983). "Issues Concerning Acquisition of Knowledge: Effects of Vocabulary Training on Reading Comprehension". *Review of Educational Research*. 53 : 2, pp. 273-79.

Morarji Desai. (1978). *Illustrated Weekly of India*. May, 2.

Morgan, B. Margaret. (1988). *Super Vocabulary*. Werner Books, New York.

Morris, J.M. (1967). *Standards and Progress in Reading*. NFER, London.

Mukherjee, S. (1990). "Fluency and Accuracy." *Education and Society*. 1 : 4 October.

Nation, I.S.P. (1974). "Techniques for Teaching Vocabulary". *English Teaching Forum*. July/September.

Nation, I.S.P. (1975). "Teaching Vocabulary in Difficult Circumstances". *English Language Teaching Journal*. 30:1, October.

Nation, I.S.P. (1983). "Testing and Teaching Vocabulary". *Guidelines*. 5 : 1.

Nation, I.S.P. and Liu Na. (1985). "Factors Affecting Guessing Vocabulary in Context". *RELC Journal*. 16 : 1, June. pp. 33-42.

Ndomba, B. (1983). "Acquiring English Vocabulary—Some Procedures and Problems". *English Teaching Forum*. April.

Nitsch, K.E. (1977). "Structuring Decontextualized forms of Knowledge". *Dissertation Abstracts International,* 38, 3935. B. (University Microfilms No. 77-30, 369).

Norman, S. (1983). "Making Vocabulary Teaching a Game". *Practical English Teaching.* 4 : 2, December.

O'Leary, F.H. (1964). "Vocabulary Presentation and Enrichment". *Elementary English.* 4 : 1 October.

O'Rourkee, Joseph Patrick. (1974). *Towards a Science of Vocabulary Development.* Monton & Co., N.U. Publishers, The Hague, Ohio.

Olson, V.A. (1965). "An Analysis of the Vocabulary of Seven Primary Reading Series". *Elementary English,* 42. pp. 261-264.

Palmberg, R. (1988). "Computer Games and Foreign Language Vocabulary Learning". *ELT Journal,* 42 : 4, October.

Patrikar, M.S. (1981). "A Linguistic Analysis of the Errors in Written English of Students of B.A. Classes of the Colleges in Urban Centres of Vidarbha". In *Third Survey of Research in Education.* Ed. M.B. Buch (1986) NCERT, New Delhi. p. 600.

Pepper, R.J. and Mayer, R.E. (1978). "Note Taking as a Generative Activity". *Journal of Educational Psychology,* 70, pp. 514-522.

Pillai, S.K. (1973). "Effects of Certain Sociological Factors on Achievement in English", *Experiments in Education,* 11 : 4, June, p. 72 & 11 : 5 July, p. 85.

Porte, G. (1988). "Poor Language Learners and their Strategies for Dealing with New Vocabulary". *ELT Journal,* 42 : 3, July, pp. 167-171.

Rajagopalan, S. (1981). "A Study of the Relationships of Selected Variables to Reading Comprehension in English". In *Third Survey of Research in Education.* Ed. M.B. Buch (1986). NCERT, New Delhi. p. 588.

Rao, R.S. (1982). "A Diagnostic Study of Reading Disability among School Children". In *Third Survey of Research in Education*. Ed. M.B. Buch (1986) NCERT, New Delhi. p. 607.

Rauf, A. (1967). *Educational Psychology*. Light and Life Publication, New Delhi.

Report of Bullock (1975). "Language for Life". Department of Education and Science. HMSO, London.

Report of the Official Language Commission (1950). Government of India, New Delhi.

Report of Kothari Commission (1964-66). Ministry of Education, Government of India, New Delhi. p. 192.

Report of the University Education Commission (1948-49). Vol. I, Manager of Publications, Delhi. p. 325.

Reutzel, D.R. and Hollingsworth, P.M. (1988). "Highlighting Key Vocabulary—A Generative Reciprocal Procedure for Teaching Selected Inference Types". *Reading Research Quarterly,* 23 : 9, pp. 358-368.

Richards, C.J. (1976). "The Role of Vocabulary Teaching". *TESOL Qtly.*, 10 : 1, March, p. 77.

Richeck, M.A. (1988). "Relating Vocabulary Learning to Word Knowledge". *Journal of Reading*. 32 : 3.

Rivers, W. (1978) *A Practical Guide to the Teaching of English*. Oxford University Press, London.

Rivers, W. (1987). *Interactive Language Teaching*. Cambridge University Press, London.

Sandosham, Linda (1980). In *Teaching Vocabulary*. By Michael Wallace (1987) ELBS. Heinemann Educational Books, London. p. 61.

Scherer, A.C. George and Michael Wertheimer (1964). *A Psycholinguistic Experiment in Foreign Language Teaching*. McGraw Hill Book Co., New York.

Schleifer, Aliah (1985). "Reaching out a Strategy for Advanced Vocabulary Acquisition". *English Teaching Forum*. April.

Schwartz, G.R. (1988). "Early Action Word Acquisition in Normal and Language Impaired Children". *Applied Psycholinguistics,* 9. pp. 111-122

Schwartz, M.R. (1988). "Learning to Learn Vocabulary in Content Area Text Books". *Journal of Reading,* 32:2.

Sen, A.L. (1983). "Teaching English Through Riddles". *English Forum,* April.

Shabbir Ahmed (1972). "Teaching and Testing Vocabulary". *English in Gujarat,* 1 : 8, September, 27. pp. 18-19.

Shah, Beena (1984) "Study of the Effect of Family Climate on Students' Academic Achievement". *The Progress of Education,* 59 : 5, p. 103.

Shah, J.H. (1979). "A Comparative Study of some Personal and Psychological Variables and Reading Comprehension". In *Third Survey of Research in Education.* Ed. M.B. Buch. (1986). NCERT, New Delhi. p. 606.

Shapiro, Jon and Lee Gunderson (1988). "A Comparison of Vocabulary Generated by Grade I Students in Whole Language Classrooms & Basal Reader Vocabulary". *Reading Research and Instruction,* 27:2. pp. 40-46.

Sharma, R.A. (1990). *Fundamentals of Educational Research.* International Publishing House, Meerut. pp. 147-153.

Sharmistha, C. (1986). "Academic Achievement of Primary School Children". *The Progress of Education,* 59 : 9, April.

Shastri, S.V. (1972). "The Teaching of English as a Second Language in Bombay with Special Reference to Structural Approach". In *Second Survey of Research in Education.* Ed. M.B. Buch (1979). Society for Educational Research and Development, Baroda.

Shaw, D.W. (1979). "English and the Indian Student". *CIEFL Bulletin,* 15 : 1.

Shukla, S.S. (1976). "Vocabulary of the Surat District Studying in Standards I to V in the age group of 6 to 11 years". In *Second Survey of Research in Education.* Ed. M.B. Buch. (1979) Society for Educational Research and Development, Baroda.

Sinha, N.K. (1975). "Active Vocabulary of Mundari Children, CIL, Mysore". In *Second Survey of Research in*

Education. Ed. M.B. Buch (1979). Society for Educational Research and Development, Baroda.

Slamecka, N.J. and Graf, P. (1978). "The Generation Effect: Delineation of a Phenomenon". *Journal of Experimental Psychology: Human Learning and Memory,* 4: pp. 592-694.

Soch, H.S. (1975). "An Investigation into the Basic Punjabi Vocabulary of Fifth Class Students in the State of Punjab". In *Second Survey of Research in Education*. Ed. M.B. Buch (1979). Society for Educational Research and Development, Baroda.

Spencer, D.H. and Jago, T.E. (1970). "The Importance of Interest in Language". *ELT Selections—I*. Ed. W.R. Lee. Oxford University Press, Oxford. p. 46.

Spolsky, B. (1969). "Attitudinal Aspects of Second Language Learning". *Language Learning,* 19 : 3&4. pp. 271-285.

Steadman, J.M. (1937). *Vocabulary Building*. Turner E. Smith & Co., Georgia.

Stenson, N. (1974). "Induced Errors". *New Frontiers in Language Learning*. Ed. John Schumann & Stenson, N., Newsbury House, Rosaley, M.A. pp. 57-70.

Subramanyam, S. (1981). *Some Correlates of Reading Achievement of Primary School Children*. Unpublished Doctoral Dissertation, Sri Venkateswara University, Tirupathi, 1981.

Tabla, H. (1967). *Teacher's Handbook for Elementary Social Studies*. Addison-Wesley, Reading, M.A.

Tejovathi, K. (1988). *Relation between English Comprehension Skills and Environmental Factors*. Unpublished Doctoral Dissertation, Nagarjuna University, Guntur.

Thames, D.G. and Readence, J.E. (1988). "Effects of Differential Vocabulary Instruction and Lesson Framework". *Reading Research and Instruction,* 27 : 2, pp. 1-12.

Underwood, B.J. and Schulz, R.W. (1960), *Meaningfulness and Verbal Learning*. Lippincott, Chicago.

Upshur, J.A. (1968). "Four Experiments on the Relation between Foreign Language Teaching and Learning". *Language Learning,* 18. pp. 111-124.

Valette, R.M. (1977). *Modern Language Testing.* Harcourt Brace Jovanovich, Inc., New York.

Wallace, J.M. (1987). *Teaching Vocabulary.* ELBS. Heinemann Educational Books, London. p. 34.

Weiss, A.S. (1986). "Differential Effects of Differing Vocabulary Presentations". *Reading Research and Instruction,* 25 : 4, pp. 265-276.

Weninger, O. (1981). "Learning Language is a Family Affair". *Education:* 102 : 2, Winter.

Wilbur, S.A. (1964). "Understanding Vocabulary of First Grade Pupils". *Elementary English,* 41 : 1, pp. 64-68.

Wilkins, D.A. (1981). *Second Language Learning and Teaching.* ELBS, London.

Wilkinson, A. (1984). "Talking and Reading in Young Children". *The Foundation of Language.* Oxford University Press, London.

Wilkinson, D. (1984). "First Impressions—Children's Knowledge of Words Gained from Single Exposure". *Applied Psycholinguistics,* 1-6.

Wittrock, M.C. (1986). Ed. *The Handbook of Research on Teaching.* Macmillan & Co., New York.

Wodinsky, M. and Nation, I.S.P. (1988). "Learning from Graded Readers". *Reading in a Foreign Language,* 5 : 1, Autumn, p. 155.

Xiaolong Li (1988). "Effects of Contextual Cues on Inferring and Remembering Meanings of New Words". *Applied Linguistics,* 9 : 4, pp. 402-413.

Yule, George. (1986). *The Study of Language.* Cambridge University Press, Cambridge.

INDEX

K

L

M

S

□□□